# THE
# HEALING
# YOUR
# ALONENESS
# WORKBOOK

# THE HEALING YOUR ALONENESS WORKBOOK

The 6-Step Inner Bonding Process

for Healing Yourself

and Your Relationships

ERIKA J. CHOPICH, PH.D.

MARGARET PAUL, PH.D.

HarperSanFrancisco

*A Division of* HarperCollins*Publishers*

For information regarding Inner Bonding therapy, lectures, and workshops, please contact:

Dr. Erika Chopich
Inner Bonding Educational Technologies
P.O. Box 5081
Santa Fe, NM 87502-5081
(505) 986-8084

Dr. Margaret Paul
Inner Bonding Educational Technologies
2531 Sawtelle Blvd. #42
Los Angeles, CA 90064
(310) 390-5993

Harper San Francisco and the authors, in association with the Rainforest Action Network, will facilitate the planting of two trees for every one tree used in the manufacture of this book.

Text design: Seventeenth Street Studios

First HarperCollins Paperback Edition Published in 1993

ISBN 0-06-250254-9

93 94  95 96 97 MAL 10 9 8 7 6 5 4 3 2 1

This edition is printed on acid-free paper that meets the American National Standards Institute Z39.48 Standard.

*To my mother "Cay," whose laughter and wonder will always be with me.*
*Thanks, Mom . . .*

Erika Chopich

*To all of my clients and to all of you who attend my workshops:*
*Thank you for the privilege of allowing me to share the miracle*
*of Inner Bonding with you.*

Margaret Paul

# Contents

# *Introduction*

The purpose of this workbook is to help you experience the Inner Bonding process. This book will teach you how to contact and get to know your core self—your Inner Child. Then you can work through the process of creating a loving relationship between your Inner Adult and your Inner Child. You will become aware of the unloving ways you are parenting your Inner Child, and it will help you begin the process of becoming a loving Adult to that Child, which is ultimately what heals the wounds of the past and brings love and joy in the present.

Inner Bonding is a profound process that, over time, creates a powerful and loving Inner Adult capable of uncovering and healing the childhood trauma and resulting false beliefs that cause our present pain. The result of Inner Bonding, of creating a loving relationship between your Adult and Inner Child, is that as your inner relationship with yourself improves, so do all your other relationships—those with your family, friends, and co-workers. Inner Bonding leads to living in love, joy, and freedom. It leads to finding your passions in life and to deepening your spirituality, your lovingness within and without. It leads to your wholeness.

The process of Inner Bonding is described in the books *Healing Your Aloneness: Creating Love and Wholeness Through Your Inner Child,* by Chopich and Paul, and *Inner Bonding,* by Paul. Reading these books is very helpful in gaining a full understanding of the Inner Bonding process but is not essential to using this workbook.

This workbook is for your personal use. The space provided is for you to write in. If you need more space to write, please just take a sheet of paper and continue, or you might consider starting an Inner Bonding journal.

If you can't answer a question because you don't know the answer or can't remember something from the past, let it go and come back to it later. As you move deeper into the Inner Bonding process, and the Inner Bond between your Adult and Child becomes more solid and loving, more information and memories will come up. Because of this you may want to go through this workbook over and over, periodically adding to what you've already discovered.

# ONE

# *Inner Bonding*

*Do you sometimes feel a sense of
aloneness and emptiness in the pit
of your stomach?*

*Do you sometimes feel lonely, even when
you are with another person or a group of
people, or even after love-making?*

Our aloneness and loneliness come from the internal disconnection between our Inner Adult and our Inner Child. Inner Bonding is the process we have developed for healing this inner split and creating our wholeness.

Essential to Inner Bonding is a basic understanding of the *terms* we will be using throughout this workbook: intent, loving behavior, Inner Child, Adult, Adult Child, false beliefs, ego, Higher Self, and codependence.

## Intent

Our intent is our most powerful motive or purpose in any given moment.[1] In our interactions with ourselves and others, we can be in only one of two intents: *to protect (avoid)* or *to learn.*The intent to protect means that we want to protect against our experience of pain and our responsibility for it. The intent to learn means that we are willing to feel our pain in order to understand how we are creating our pain and that we want responsibility for healing past pain, for taking action to relieve present pain, and for bringing ourselves joy. At any given moment, we are either in the intent to protect and avoid or in the intent to learn.

## Loving Behavior

We are behaving lovingly when we take full responsibility for our pain and joy, and when we nurture and support our own and others' emotional and spiritual growth. The intent to learn is loving behavior; when we are in the intent to protect, we are behaving unlovingly to ourselves and others.

## Inner Child

Our Inner Child is who we are when we are born, our natural or core self: our natural feelings, personality, sense of humor, softness, talents, wisdom, creativity, playfulness, intuition, curiosity, spontaneity, sensitivity, sensuality, and sense of wonder. Our Child is our right-brain inner experience as felt through our bodies, our "gut" response.

In any given moment, our Inner Child feels either loved or unloved by us, our Adult self. When our Child is feeling loved, we are able to flow with our creativity, passion, and joy, but when our Child is feeling unloved by our Adult, our Child feels alone inside, empty, lonely, sad, shamed, anxious, scared, panicked, and depressed. Our Child feels

---

1. For a deeper understanding in intent, see Paul, Jordan and Margaret, *Do I Have To Give Up Me To Be Loved By You? The Workbook* (Formerly – *From Conflict to Caring* Minneapolis: CompCare, 1989), *Do I Have To Give Up Me To Be Loved By My Kids?* (Minneapolis: CompCare, 1987), and *Do I Have To Give Up Me To Be Loved By You?* (Minneapolis: CompCare, 1983).

unloved by us when we do not take responsibility for our own pain and joy.

Understanding what our Inner Child needs to feel loved by us through the intent to learn, and then taking the action necessary to heal past and present pain and bring about joy, is the heart of Inner Bonding. Inner Bonding is a profoundly creative process that allows us to move ever deeper into becoming truly loving and joyful human beings.

## Adult

Our Adult is our accumulation of learned knowledge—our intellect, our left-brain, logical, analytical, conscious mind. The Adult is concerned primarily with thought and action, with doing rather than with being, feeling, and experiencing, which are the realms of the Child. Our Adult is our outer aspect of action while our Child is our inner aspect of experience. Our Adult aspect is the choice maker regarding our intent and resulting actions; that is, our Adult chooses the intent to learn or the intent to protect. Just as in a family the adults decide how they are going to treat their children—whether they will protect through authoritarian (controlling) or permissive (neglectful or indulgent) parenting, or be open to learning about their children and how best to love them—so our Inner Adult or Parent makes this decision regarding our intent toward our own Inner Child.

The loving Adult is the part of us that is connected to universal love and truth. It is the part of us through which flows the energy to take loving action in behalf of our Inner Child. The loving Adult is always in the intent to learn.

## Adult Child

From the moment of our birth, we begin to develop our Adult from watching the adults around us. We develop our concept of how to act in the world toward ourselves and others by watching how our parents and other caregivers treat themselves and by experiencing how they treat us. Our Adult learns to be loving or unloving to ourselves and others from our role models: our parents, siblings, grandparents, other relatives, friends, teachers, religious leaders, and from books, movies, and TV. Most of us learned to protect ourselves against our pain through substance and process addictions, through overtly controlling behavior (blaming anger, threats, criticism, shaming, violence, and so on), through covertly controlling behavior (caretaking, teaching, compliance, flattery, seductiveness), and through resistance (procrastination, incompetence, forgetting, withdrawal). We have not met anyone who grew up observing and experiencing their parents or anyone else in the intent to learn about themselves, their mates and children, or about universal truth and love. Because we have not had any role modeling in the intent to learn, most of us find this simple concept to be an enormous challenge in our everyday lives.

Our Adult Child, the unloving Adult that our unloved Child learned to be, is the part of us that was patterned after the Adult Child of our parents or other caregivers. Many of us had to take adult responsibility very early in our lives because our parents were abusive or absent. This Adult Child that we developed at such a young age to take care of our parents and ourselves is our abandoned Child, the part of ourselves that is filled with pain and false beliefs. Our Adult Child attempts to numb this pain through addictions and through codependent or violent behavior. Our Adult Child operates from different ages, depending on the situation. Sometimes it is 2 years old, or 10 years old, or a teenager.

The Adult Child is always in the intent to protect and is therefore incapable of loving, unable to explore our pain and the false beliefs that create our pain.

Most of us have never developed a true Adult, a loving Inner Parent who knows how to love and nurture our Inner Child and love others without compliant and controlling behavior. Inner Bonding is about developing that loving Inner Adult.

## False Beliefs

A false belief is a belief about ourselves or others that causes us fear. Our false beliefs, such as a belief that we are unlovable, cause much of our pain; our false beliefs cause much of our behavior, such as our controlling behavior, that often results in pain. If we believe we are unlovable, unworthy, or unimportant, then we will generally behave in ways that create rejection. Our false beliefs are the lies we have learned about ourselves and others that cause our fear and anxiety. Our false beliefs lie within our Adult Child.

## Ego

Inner Bonding uses the definition of ego described in *A Course of Miracles* and in Eastern philosophy. The ego is the false self, the constructed personality that we create out of our shame-based false belief that we are bad, wrong, unlovable, unworthy, inadequate, unimportant, or flawed. Our ego is the home of our false beliefs, the seat of the lies that create our fear and shame. It is the result of our disconnection from ourselves and therefore from a Higher Power. Our ego was formed from the false conclusions we drew when we didn't receive the love we needed as small children and created a false self in an effort to get that love. *Our ego is our Adult Child.*

## Higher Self

The Higher Self is who we are in a connected state, a state in which the loving Adult and the Inner Child are Inner Bonded. When our Adult bonds with the Inner Child through the intent to learn, the heart opens and we can give and receive love in communion with others and with our Higher Power. Our Higher Self is connected to the truths of the universe and operates from love and faith rather than from fear and shame. Our Higher Self is the channel through which our Higher Power speaks to us. Sometimes our Higher Power speaks to us through our loved Child, our gut or feeling process, and sometimes through our loving Adult, our mind or thought process. It is the inner-bonded, connected state, the Higher Self state, that opens the channel to Higher Wisdom.

## Codependence

We define codependence as being *externally referented,* that is, defining ourselves from outside ourselves. When we hand the power to define ourselves over to other people, when other people's approval or disapproval is allowed to determine our worth and lovability, we are codependent.

The above terms will become clearer as you read and work through this workbook.

### The Six-Step Inner Bonding Process

Inner Bonding is a six-step process, and each step requires certain skills. The purpose of this workbook is to teach you the skills necessary to work through these six steps, which can lead you from inner conflict to inner peace and joy, and from external conflict with others to love and connection. The six steps are:

1. Awareness of some inner discomfort or pain: tension, anxiety, fear, shame, disappointment, grief, sadness, aloneness, emptiness, loneliness, anger, depression, terror, panic. We cannot begin to learn about and heal those feelings until we know we have them. Yet, many of us are so adept at protecting against our pain with substance and process addictions that we protect before we are even aware of our pain.

2. The Adult chooses the intent to learn about the discomfort or pain.

3. The Adult dialogues with the Inner Child to learn the source of the pain. This dialogue includes exploring the false beliefs with the Adult Child that cause our pain and discovering the past experiences that created our beliefs. During the dialogue process the Adult allows the Child to vent anger and release grief.

4. The Adult dialogues with his or her Higher Power to discover the truth about the false beliefs and to find the loving behavior toward the Inner Child.

5. The Adult takes the necessary loving action to heal the past and present pain and bring about joy and fulfillment.

6. The Adult evaluates the action to see if it is meeting the Child's needs by tuning in to the consequences of the action.

The exercises in this workbook are designed to:

- Help you become aware of the feelings of your Inner Child.

- Teach you how to move into the intent to learn.

- Teach you how to dialogue with your Inner Child, your Adult Child, and your Higher Power.

- Teach you how to develop your loving Adult.

- Teach you how to lovingly take care of your own Inner Child when alone and with others.

By working through these exercises you will gain the skills you need to use Inner Bonding whenever you need it, that is, whenever you are experiencing discomfort or pain.

Chart 1, adapted from *Inner Bonding,* outlines this six-step process. As you go deeper and deeper with each step, the process will become real, personal, and operational.

## Chart 1: The Paths Through Inner Conflict

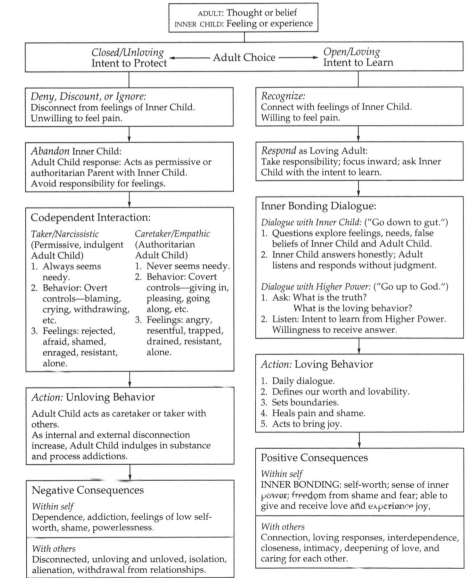

ADULT: Thought or belief
INNER CHILD: Feeling or experience

*Closed/Unloving*
Intent to Protect ← Adult Choice → *Open/Loving*
Intent to Learn

*Deny, Discount, or Ignore:*
Disconnect from feelings of Inner Child.
Unwilling to feel pain.

*Recognize:*
Connect with feelings of Inner Child.
Willing to feel pain.

*Abandon* Inner Child:
Adult Child response: Acts as permissive or authoritarian Parent with Inner Child.
Avoid responsibility for feelings.

*Respond* as Loving Adult:
Take responsibility; focus inward; ask Inner Child with the intent to learn.

Codependent Interaction:

*Taker/Narcissistic*
(Permissive, indulgent Adult Child)
1. Always seems needy.
2. Behavior: Overt controls—blaming, crying, withdrawing, etc.
3. Feelings: rejected, afraid, shamed, enraged, resistant, alone.

*Caretaker/Empathic*
(Authoritarian Adult Child)
1. Never seems needy.
2. Behavior: Covert controls—giving in, pleasing, going along, etc.
3. Feelings: angry, resentful, trapped, drained, resistant, alone.

Inner Bonding Dialogue:

*Dialogue with Inner Child:* ("Go down to gut.")
1. Questions explore feelings, needs, false beliefs of Inner Child and Adult Child.
2. Inner Child answers honestly; Adult listens and responds without judgment.

*Dialogue with Higher Power:* ("Go up to God.")
1. Ask: What is the truth?
          What is the loving behavior?
2. Listen: Intent to learn from Higher Power. Willingness to receive answer.

*Action:* Loving Behavior

1. Daily dialogue.
2. Defines our worth and lovability.
3. Sets boundaries.
4. Heals pain and shame.
5. Acts to bring joy.

*Action:* Unloving Behavior

Adult Child acts as caretaker or taker with others.
As internal and external disconnection increase, Adult Child indulges in substance and process addictions.

Negative Consequences

*Within self*
Dependence, addiction, feelings of low self-worth, shame, powerlessness.

*With others*
Disconnected, unloving and unloved, isolation, alienation, withdrawal from relationships.

Positive Consequences

*Within self*
INNER BONDING: self-worth; sense of inner power; freedom from shame and fear; able to give and receive love and experience joy.

*With others*
Connection, loving responses, interdependence, closeness, intimacy, deepening of love, and caring for each other.

# TWO

# Discovering Your Inner Child

Many of us have ignored our Inner Child for so long that we are not even sure we have one inside. We have so completely disconnected from our feelings that we are out of touch with the feeling part of ourselves. You cannot begin the process of lovingly parenting your Inner Child until you know you have a Child and develop an idea of who that Child is. At the beginning of discovering your Inner Child, it is often helpful to playact or make up your Inner Child if you aren't sure that the voice you hear is that of your Child. Learning to distinguish between the Adult voice and the Child voice takes time and practice.

## Introducing Yourself to Your Child

As a prelude to discovering your Inner Child, it is often helpful to introduce yourself to your Child, just as you would if you were adopting yourself as an actual child. Following is an example of a short introductory letter. Your letter can be as long or as short as you want.

### Sample Letter of Introduction from Adult to Child

*Hello, little one, I'm your Inner Parent. I haven't paid much attention to you for a very long time. I guess I've put a lid on you because you scare me. I think you're the one who got me into lots of trouble when I was little. I know you need my love and caring, and I'm going to learn in this workbook how to feel you and hear you and give you what you need. I want to learn what it means to love you. I've tried to get everyone else to love you, and now it's my turn to learn to give you what you need. I know I haven't been very nice to you. I haven't been there when you hurt and I've told you bad things about yourself, but now I want to learn to love you. I don't really know you yet, but I would like to know you. I hope you will let me in. I don't blame you if you are angry or afraid of me, but I hope you will let me in on those feelings. Even if you are silent and don't want to talk to me, I will still learn what it means to love you.*

Now write your own letter of introduction to your Inner Child. Use an extra sheet of paper if you need more room.

## Beginning to Discover Your Child

The following exercise will help you begin to distinguish between your Child and your Adult. You may not be able to answer all the questions; just do as many as you can. Some of the questions may have the same answer; that is, your Adult and your Child may have some of the same likes and dislikes.

§ Imagine walking into a video shop and picking out two videos—one for your Child and one for your Adult.

What would you pick for your Child? _____

_____

What would you pick for your Adult? _____

_____

§ Imagine sitting in a restaurant, looking at a menu, and picking out one dish for your Child and one for your Adult.

What would you pick for your Child? _____

What would you pick for your Adult? _____

§ Imagine walking into a large bookstore and buying a book for your Child to read and a book for your Adult to read.

What would you choose for your Child? _____

What would you choose for your Adult? _____

§ Imagine going into a music store and buying a cassette or disk for your Child and one for your Adult.

What would you choose for your Child? _____

What would you choose for your Adult? _____

§ Imagine that you are going to spend the evening watching a TV show.

If your Child were to select the show, what show would it be?

_____

If your Adult were to select the show, what show would it be?

_____

§ Think about the people you know and spend time with.

Whom does your Child like the best? _____

Whom does your Adult like the best? _____

§ What kind of people does your Child value the most?_____

_____

_____

What kind of people does your Adult value the most? _____

_____

_____

§ If you were to give yourself a play day:

What would your Child like to do? _____

_____

What would your Adult like to do? _____

_____

How does your Child feel about the work you do? _____

_____

_____

How does your Adult feel about the work you do? _____

_____

_____

§ If you could choose at this moment any work you wanted to do:

What work would your Child choose? _____

_____

What work would your Adult choose? _____

_____

What kind of clothes does your Child like? _____

_____

What kind of clothes does your Adult like? _____

_____

What is your Child's favorite color? _____

_____

What is your Adult's favorite color? _____

_____

Hopefully, this exercise has helped you begin to realize that there really are two distinct parts of you. If you were not able to answer many of the questions, take heart. Put the questions aside and go back to them later, after you have had more experience with your Inner Child.

## Visualization to Contact Your Inner Child

The following visualization can be read silently to yourself, or you can have someone read it to you. Reading it to soft music can help you relax and remember. Sit in a comfortable chair as you go through this visualization.

*Settle comfortably into your chair. . . . If someone is reading to you, close your eyes. . . . Take some deep, relaxing breaths, and as you exhale, let all tension go. . . . Notice which part of your body is most tight—legs, chest, shoulders, forehead. Breathe into it and just let go. . . . Let your shoulders drop, . . . let your jaw relax, . . . unclench your teeth, . . . let the chair support your body totally, . . . let your body be very relaxed.*

*Allow your mind to go backwards in time, backwards to a painful event in childhood, a time when you felt hurt or frightened and were alone with these feelings. Perhaps you remember a particular event, such as being punished by a parent or rejected by a friend or humiliated in some way, or just a general sense of sadness and aloneness. . . .*

*See yourself as a child alone in your room, or alone where you would go when you were hurting. See yourself lonely and in pain. . . .*

*Now, see yourself as a grown-up, as you are now, coming into the room. . . . Introduce yourself to the child. See yourself as a child looking in wonder at you as an adult. Sit down next to yourself as a child and proceed to become the most loving Adult you can imagine—holding, stroking, talking, reassuring, hearing the pain. Put yourself as a child onto your lap, holding your Child close to you.*

*Feel the fear, sadness, and aloneness slowly drain away as your Child feels you there with your love.*

*Let your Child know that you will always be there for him or her, now that you are grown up—that you will be there for the fear and pain and sadness and hurt, that you will be there to bring your Child joy.*

*Now pull your Child into you, into your middle—pulling in all his or her feelings, aliveness, passion, knowingness, sweetness, goodness, pain, fear, anger, joy. . . . Feel your Child within you.*

*Now take a few deep breaths and bring yourself back into the present, bringing your Child with you, bringing all the feelings with you.*

### Connecting to the Feelings of Your Child

The very first step of the Inner Bonding process is awareness of feelings. For those of us who have spent years avoiding our feelings, this first step can be a big challenge. Before we go into how to connect, it is helpful to become aware of how you protect against feeling your feelings. All of us learned from parents and peers many ways to protect against our painful feelings. What are the ways you, as an Adult Child, have learned to avoid or numb your painful feelings? Anything that we do to excess can be a way to fill the inner emptiness and numb the pain and fear. Anything outside of ourselves that we use to make ourselves feel adequate and lovable, or to avoid pain, is an addiction.

Go through the following list and check off the ways you protect against feeling your pain:

### Substance Addictions

❏ Food

❏ Binging, purging

❏ Sugar

❏ Cigarettes

❏ Caffeine

❏ Drugs

❏ Alcohol

❏ Busyness

## Process Addictions: Things and Activities

❏ TV

❏ Work

❏ Reading

❏ Sports

❏ Anorexia

❏ Exercise

❏ Power

❏ Gambling

❏ Money

❏ Spending

❏ Sleep

❏ Shoplifting

❏ Ruminating

❏ Worry

❏ Misery

❏ Talking

❏ Meditation

❏ Talking on the telephone

❏ Drama

❏ Danger

❏ Glamour

❏ Religion

### Process Addictions: People

❏ Sex

❏ Romance

❏ Love

❏ Approval

Turning to these substance and process addictions can make it impossible to connect to your feelings. If you are serious about Inner Bonding and about learning to be a loving Adult to your Inner Child, then you need to face the possibility that your addictions are keeping you from connecting to yourself.

### Connecting to Your Feelings

Your Child communicates to you through your body. After all, feelings are merely physical sensations to which we have attached words. Just as your body tells you when you are hungry, thirsty, or tired, so it tells you that you are sad, angry, frightened, loving, or excited. You may get a lump in your throat when you are moved; perhaps your heart feels large and full when you feel love; maybe your stomach starts to grind or your legs get rubbery when you are frightened; your neck or shoulders may tighten when you are anxious; maybe you feel shivers or tears in your eyes when you feel truth.

Many of us disconnected from our bodies as children because the physical and emotional pain we felt was too great to handle. Some of us even learned to leave our bodies as a way of handling the extreme abuse that was inflicted upon us. As we grew older, we learned to protect ourselves in other ways, such as through the substance and process addictions listed above. To become a loving Adult to our Inner Child, however, we must reconnect with our bodies so that we can be aware of our feelings. Spend a few minutes now tuning into your body as you answer the following questions. Move your focus down into your body, into your gut, your legs, your hands, your heart, your neck and shoulders, and *feel* where you feel your feelings.

§ Where in your body do you feel your anger? How do you know when you are angry?

_____

_____

_____

§ Where do you feel your anxiety?

_____

_____

_____

§ Where do you feel your hurt?

_____

_____

_____

§ Where do you feel your sadness?

_____

_____

_____

§ Where do you feel your fear?

_____

_____

_____

§ Where do you feel your aloneness?

_____

_____

_____

§ Where do you feel your loneliness?

_____

_____

_____

§ Where do you feel your grief?

_____

_____

_____

§ Where do you feel your joy?

_____

_____

_____

§ Where do you feel your excitement?

_____

_____

_____

§ Where do you feel your peacefulness?

_____

_____

_____

§ Where do you feel your caring?

_____

_____

_____

§ Where do you feel your love?

_____

_____

_____

§ Where do you feel your sense of knowing the truth?

_____

_____

_____

If you find that you are unable to answer many of these questions, you may be blocked within your body. Some form of bodywork, such as neo-Reichian work or rebirthing, guided breathing techniques that open the body to feelings, is often very helpful in releasing the blocks within the body. Until you are aware of your feelings, you will find it very difficult to dialogue with your Inner Child and your Higher Power, which is the heart of the Inner Bonding process.

Earlier in this chapter you wrote a letter of introduction from your Adult to your Inner Child. Now it's time to allow your Child to write to you, introducing himself or herself. Below is an example of a letter written by little Tommy to Adult Tom:

**Sample Letter from Child to Adult**

*Hi.*

*I'm Tommy. I need you. Please listen to me. I try to tell you things all the time. I even make your stomach hurt so you will listen to me, but you just take pills to make me go away. I'm scared a lot and I feel very alone. Please notice me. I need you to love me. I like that you wrote to me but I'm afraid you will go away again. Don't go away. I love you and I'm also mad at you. Please listen to me and talk to me.*

*Love,*

*Tommy*

Now write your own letter to your Adult. As you write this letter, move your focus into your body, particularly into your gut. Allow yourself to feel like a small child, and write the letter with your *nondominant hand*.

_____

_____

_____

_____

_____

_____

_____

_____

_____

_____

_____

_____

_____

_____

_____

_____

_____

_____

_____

_____

_____

## How Do You Feel About Your Inner Child?

Your feelings about your Inner Child are determined by the many experiences you had as you were growing up—primarily how your parents, siblings, grandparents, or other caregivers treated you, each other, and themselves. Becoming aware of your feelings about children in general may help you get in touch with your feelings about your own Inner Child.

Some of you had two parents. Some of you had one, and some of you had none. Where we use the terms *mother* and *father*, please substitute the name of whoever was your primary caregiver.

## How Your Parents or Other Caregivers Felt About Children and About You

§ How do you think your mother felt about children in general?

_____

_____

_____

_____

_____

_____

_____

§ How do you think your father felt about children in general?

_____

_____

_____

_____

_____

_____

_____

§ How do you think your mother felt about her own children?

_____

_____

_____

_____

_____

_____

_____

§ How do you think your father felt about his own children?

_____

_____

_____

_____

_____

_____

_____

§ How do you think your mother felt about you?

_____

_____

_____

_____

_____

_____

_____

§ How do you think your father felt about you?

_____

_____

_____

_____

_____

_____

_____

§ Did one or both of your parents believe that "children should be seen and not heard"?

_____

_____

_____

_____

_____

_____

_____

§ Did one or both of your parents believe in "Spare the rod and spoil the child"?

_____

_____

_____

_____

_____

_____

_____

## How You Feel About Children

§ How do you feel about children? Do you like them? Dislike them? Are you indifferent to them? Annoyed by them?

_____

_____

_____

_____

_____

_____

§ If you like children, what about them appeals to you the most?

_____

_____

_____

_____

_____

_____

§ What about children appeals to you the least? Do they make too much noise? Are they too needy? Too demanding? In the way, a bother?

_____

_____

_____

_____

_____

_____

§ Why do you think people have children?

_____

_____

_____

_____

_____

_____

## Your Beliefs About Children

§ Do you believe children are born "blank," a clean slate, ready to be taught and acted upon, but with no inherent ways of being?

_____

_____

_____

_____

_____

_____

_____

§ Do you believe children are born with inherent wisdom, emotions, talents, ways of being?

_____

_____

_____

_____

_____

_____

_____

§ Do you believe children are born loving, unloving, good, evil, neutral?

_____

_____

_____

_____

_____

_____

_____

§ Do you believe that "children should be seen and not heard"?

_____

_____

_____

_____

_____

_____

_____

§ Do you believe in "Spare the rod and spoil the child"?

_____

_____

_____

_____

_____

_____

_____

§ Do you believe that children are born equal to adults in their humanity and their rights? Are children less important than adults? Are they more important than adults?

_____

_____

_____

_____

_____

_____

_____

§ Do you believe that small children are capable of thinking for themselves? Can they know what they want? Can they know how they feel?

_____

_____

_____

_____

_____

_____

_____

§ Do you believe that children have something to offer adults? If so, what do they have to offer? If not, why not?

_____

_____

_____

_____

_____

_____

_____

৯ How do your feelings about children compare with your parents' feelings about children?

_____

_____

_____

_____

_____

_____

Many of the exercises in the following chapters will help you get to know your Inner Child on deeper and deeper levels, and as you do, your feelings about your Inner Child will change. Some of you have worked extensively with your Inner Child and some of you are just beginning, but all of you have some beliefs and feelings about your Inner Child.

৯ What are your beliefs and feelings about your Inner Child?

_____

_____

_____

_____

_____

_____

_____

_____

_____

After working through this workbook, come back to what you have just written and see if your beliefs and feelings have changed.

# THREE

# *Codependence vs. Wholeness:*

## What Determines the Difference in How Your Inner Child Feels?

From the time we are very small we are given the unspoken message that if we follow a certain path, or do the things we are expected to do, we will somehow create a happy life. These messages and beliefs come from our parents and family, as well as from teachers, books, movies, and television.

Recall whether your parents pushed you to do well in school and why or why not. How did they respond to the people you dated? Did your family watch television shows like "Ozzie and Harriet," "Leave It to Beaver," and "The Waltons"? Were your parents concerned with how you dressed? Were they themselves image-conscious? All the unspoken messages came together to help us adopt a belief system regarding how we arrive at joy. The "magic recipe" looks something like this:

+ graduate from high school

+ graduate from college

+ land the "right" job

+ marry the "right" person

+ have perfect children

+ live in the best house in the best neighborhood

+ drive the "right" car

+ own the best of everything

+ never divorce

---

**the Sum Total** = peace and happiness for the rest of your life!

Accepting the idea that self-esteem and joy come from things and people outside ourselves is what we call being *externally referenced.* This is the definition of codependence—the belief that our worth, self-esteem, joy, and pain come from outside ourselves, from the things, people, and events in our lives. Those holding the opposite belief, that pain and joy, as well as a sense of worth and lovability, come from within, are said to be *internally referenced.* For example, if you were to sit in a chair in your living room with no distractions for an extended period of time, say three hours, how would you feel at the end of that time? Bored? Anxious? Sleepy? Peaceful? Calm? Happy?

If left alone with nothing but your thoughts, you begin to get the idea that *all* your feelings come from within. That is, our belief system creates our thoughts, but our thoughts create our feelings! *That* is being internally referenced. Unfortunately, most people are codependent, or externally referenced, believing that all their good and painful feelings come from outside themselves. They have handed the job of self-definition to others instead of accepting that job themselves.

The following process will help you determine your reference and the intensity with which you believe in it. Rate each of the statements below on a scale of 0 to 5 (5 = always true for me; 0 = never true for me).

1. _____ I enjoy my new car only when other people see it.

2. _____ I believe I look good only when I receive compliments.

3. _____ I feel humiliated if others see my house messy.

4. _____ I feel shamed by my mistakes.

5. _____ My best feelings come from the approval of others.

6. _____ Winning is important to me.

7. _____ I have to be the best at everything.

8. _____ I feel lonely when I am alone.

9. _____ I worry about making a fool of myself.

10. _____ I love to be seen as generous and philanthropic.

11. _____ I always feel left out.

12. _____ I can't be alone. I am afraid to be alone.

13. _____ My pain comes from others' behavior.

14. _____ My anger comes from others' behavior, and I am justified in being angry when others let me down.

15. _____ I feel powerless over my feelings—over my own pain and joy.

16. _____ I feel responsible for the feelings of others. Their pain is my fault, and it's my responsibility to make others happy.

_____ **Total Score** (80 possible)

Again, rate the following on a scale of 0 to 5 (5 = always true for me; 0 = never true for me).

1. _____ I enjoy alone time.

2. _____ I have many hobbies.

3. _____ I enjoy my creativity.

4. _____ Spirituality is important to me.

5. _____ I value my body, health, and well-being.

6. _____ I can laugh at myself.

7. _____ I am the only one responsible for my feelings of hurt, pain, and joy.

8. _____ I get pleasure out of others' joy.

9. _____ I am generally aware of my feelings and my responsibility for them.

10. _____ I feel rich and whole just walking in the woods.

11. _____ I am deeply aware of my own goodness, worth, and lovability and it's okay if others don't see those qualities.

12. _____ I can feel inner peace even when doing mundane tasks.

13. _____ I do not feel responsible for the feelings of others.

14. _____ I am willing to lose others rather than lose myself.

15. _____ I have the power to make myself happy.

16. _____ I am open to learning about my own feelings and needs and open to learning about other people's feelings and needs.

_____ **Total Score** (80 possible)

Now compare your two scores. First List _____ Second List _____

If you scored higher on the first list, you are probably codependent. A higher score on the second list indicates wholeness. Like many people, you may find that your scores on the two lists are nearly equal. The idea is to begin to understand how you are most motivated.

*All* healing processes require a shift from external to internal motivation and reference. Inner Bonding is no exception. To determine whether we are a loving Adult to ourselves we must begin to move our eyes inward, taking a careful survey and assuming responsibility for all that we see and everything that we experience. This means letting go of blame (external reference; intent to protect) and replacing it with concern for how best to care for our Inner Child in any situation (internal reference; intent to learn). This is a core step in determining what your Inner Child will feel. This is your Adult's "job."

When we were small, our definition of ourselves had to come from outside ourselves, from our parents, teachers, and other caregivers. Because little children have not been on the planet long enough to have a well-defined, loving Inner Adult, they cannot define themselves. It was the job of our caregivers to hold up an accurate mirror so that we could learn to know who we truly are. If the adults around us did not see us as worthy and lovable, we learned to believe that we are unworthy and unlovable. If they saw us as bad, wrong, in the way, incompetent; if our feelings and needs were unimportant to them and they neglected us; if they violated us with hitting, yelling, shaming, or sexual abuse, then we developed core shame-based beliefs about ourselves that still operate today. Once we define ourselves as bad, wrong, unworthy, unlovable, incompetent, unimportant, or flawed, we naturally look outside ourselves for the love and approval we so desperately need. We become addicted to outside approval for our good feelings, which is what codependence is. As with any addiction, we need a constant supply of approval to feel okay, and we instantly feel bad when we receive disapproval. We will always take others' disapproval personally when it links up with our own shame-based definition of ourselves. Because our feelings go up and down according to whether we are receiving love and approval, we naturally come to believe that our feelings—our pain and joy—come from outside ourselves. We come to believe that we cannot handle the loss of love and approval—that it is too painful, even life-threatening. Our codependent behavior comes from these false beliefs.

What are your false beliefs about your happiness and self-esteem? Check the beliefs that your Adult Child thinks are true.

❏ My adequacy, lovability, and feelings of self-worth and self-esteem come from others liking me and approving of me.

❏ My sense of happiness and well-being comes from another loving me.

❏ Other people's disapproval or rejection means that I am not good enough.

❏ I can't make myself happy.

❏ I can't make myself as happy as someone or something else can.

❏ My best feelings come from outside myself, from how others (or a particular other) see me and treat me.

## Takers and Caretakers

Codependent behavior falls into two distinct categories: the *narcissistic* behavior of *takers* and the *empathic* behavior of *caretakers.* In any given relationship we may find ourselves in one category with some issues and in the other category with other issues. Or we may be in one category in one relationship and in the other category in a different relationship. Virtually all of us function in both these categories some of the time, and in one of these categories most of the time. We have never known a client or friend who did not exhibit some codependent behavior. All of us suffered some physical, emotional, or sexual abuse that led to the shame-based beliefs that create codependence.

Wanting the love and approval of others, we naturally try to obtain some control over getting it. Our overt and covert controlling codependent behavior is based on our false beliefs about control. What are your beliefs about control? Check the statements that your Adult Child believes are true:

❏ I can control how others feel about me and treat me.

❏ I can control whether people like me, love me, care about me, respect me.

❑ I can have control over whether people reject me.

❑ I can have control over someone desiring me sexually.

❑ I can have control over people doing what I want.

Two codependent people create a codependent system, generally with one person as the taker, on the narcissistic side of codependence, and the other as the caretaker, on the empathic side. As you go through the exercises about these categories, it will be helpful if you are open to learning rather than shaming yourself and others as you recognize ways in which you and others behave.

Throughout this section, check off the beliefs that your Adult Child thinks are true. Note that the word *partner* is used in these exercises to refer to any relationship with a mate, lover, child, parent, friend, or co-worker.  You can go through this list and answer it several times with different relationships in mind.

## Taker (Narcissistic Behavior)

❑ My partner is responsible for my feelings, needs, and behavior.

❑ My partner is responsible for making me feel safe, worthy, and lovable.

❑ My partner is responsible for my anger or other forms of acting out when he or she doesn't give me what I want and need.

❑ If someone cares about me, that person will never do anything that hurts or upsets me.

❑ My needs should be more important to my partner than his or her own needs.

❑ Others are selfish if they do what they want instead of what I want or need.

❑ If my partner really loved me, he or she would generally put my needs first.

❑ When I'm hurt or upset, it's someone else's fault.

❑ It's up to other people to make me feel good about myself by approving of me.

❑ I'm not responsible for causing my feelings. Other people make me feel happy, sad, angry, frustrated, shut down, or depressed. When I'm angry, someone makes me feel that way and is responsible for fixing my feelings.

❑ I'm not responsible for my behavior. Other people make me yell, act crazy, get sick, laugh, cry, get violent, leave, or fail.

❑ I can't take care of myself. I need someone to take care of me.

❑ I can't be alone. I feel like I'll die if I'm alone.

❑ I can make my partner love me, see me, hear me, and approve of me with my controlling behavior (see the list below for overtly controlling behavior), and it is my right to impose this control to get my needs met.

When we are on the taker end of the codependent system, our Adult Child attempts to control in various overt ways. In what ways do you attempt to control? Put a check mark next to the behaviors that apply to you, and try to stay open to learning, not judging yourself for the things you do. You cannot learn what you do if you are judging yourself, and you cannot change what you do if you don't know that you are doing it.

§ I attempt to get my way or get love and approval with:

**Verbal Shaming**

❑ Criticizing

❑ Judging

❑ Belittling

❑ Taunting

❑ Put-downs

❑ Scolding

❑ Making comparisons

❑ Sarcasm

❑ Teasing

### Nonverbal Shaming

❏ Saying "Tsk, tsk" and shaking head

❏ Raising eyebrows

❏ Scowling

❏ Shrugging shoulders

❏ Rolling eyes

❏ Disapproving looks

❏ Disapproving sighs

### Other Forms of Control

❏ Yelling

❏ Blaming anger

❏ Temper tantrums

❏ Rage

❏ Getting annoyed, irritated, short, curt

❏ Silent angry withdrawal, the silent treatment

❏ Accusing, blaming

❏ Interrogating

❏ Pouting, sulking

❏ Blaming tears, "poor me" tears

❏ Telling feelings with hurt and blame

❏ Complaining, whining

❏ Becoming ill

❏ Being sneaky, deceptive

❏ Lying

❏ Withholding the truth

- ❏ Telling half-truths
- ❏ Changing the subject, interrupting
- ❏ Therapizing, analyzing, interpreting
- ❏ Pushing others into therapy
- ❏ Nagging
- ❏ Moralizing
- ❏ Lecturing
- ❏ Giving advice, teaching
- ❏ Becoming self-righteous, having a superior attitude
- ❏ Acting like a know-it-all
- ❏ Explaining, justifying
- ❏ Convincing, selling
- ❏ Denying
- ❏ Arguing
- ❏ Talking others out of their feelings by telling them they are wrong
- ❏ Asking leading questions to which only one answer is acceptable
- ❏ Bribery
- ❏ Hitting, spanking, beating
- ❏ Throwing things
- ❏ Breaking things, destroying things
- ❏ Torturing
- ❏ Raping and other sexual abuse

## Using Threats of:

- ❏ Financial withdrawal
- ❏ Emotional withdrawal
- ❏ Sexual withdrawal

❏ Exposure to others

❏ Abandonment, physical withdrawal

❏ Illness

❏ Violence

❏ Suicide

❏ Alcohol or drug abuse

❏ Having a nervous breakdown

❏ Having a heart attack or stroke

❧ When I don't get my way and get the behavior, love, or approval I want, I feel:

❏ Rejected

❏ Abandoned

❏ Frightened

❏ Hurt

❏ Victimized

❏ Alone

❏ Needy

❏ Inadequate, wrong

❏ Unlovable, unworthy

❏ Resistant

❏ Angry

❏ Enraged, out of control

❏ Anxious

❏ Ill

❏ Suicidal

❏ Empty

❏ Numb

❏ Righteous

When we are on the taker or narcissistic end of the codependent cycle we are behaving from our young Adult Child, with no loving Adult to set limits on the behavior and take responsibility for our feelings.

### Caretaker (Empathic Behavior)

Now, place a check mark next to the items below that apply to you.

§ In a relationship with a mate, lover, child, parent, friend, or co-worker, I believe that:

❏ I am responsible for my partner's good feelings—for making my partner feel safe, happy, worthy, and lovable.

❏ When I care about someone, it's my responsibility to make that person happy.

❏ My partner's feelings of hurt, pain, and anger are my fault, and it's my responsibility to do something about it.

❏ If other people are angry at me, I made them feel that way and I'm responsible for fixing their feelings.

❏ Since I'm responsible for my partner's feelings, I should never do anything that hurts or upsets my partner, even if it's something that makes me happy and is not intended to hurt anyone.

❏ If I don't take responsibility for my partner's happiness and unhappiness, I'm not a caring person.

❏ If I take responsibility for my own happiness instead of putting others first, I'm being selfish.

❏ My worth is in making others happy.

❏ Other people's needs and feelings are more important than mine.

❏ I can get the love and approval of others with my covertly controlling behavior. (See list below of covertly controlling behavior.)

§ I attempt to gain approval and avoid disapproval, through covert control, by:

❏ Being "nice," even when I don't mean it

❏ Giving gifts with strings attached

❏ Being emotionally or financially indispensable

❏ Flattering people or giving false compliments

❏ Giving in, giving myself up, going along

❏ Not asking for what I want, putting aside what I want

❏ Agreeing with others' points of view

❏ People-pleasing

❏ Rescuing

❏ Censoring what I say about what I want and feel

❏ Second-guessing and anticipating what others want

❏ Putting myself down

❏ Being seductive

§ When my caretaking doesn't work to get me the love and approval I want, I feel:

❏ Angry

❏ Resentful

❏ Used

❏ Drained

❏ Trapped

❏ Engulfed

❏ Alone

❏ Resistant

❏ Unappreciated

❏ Frustrated

❏ Depressed

People on the caretaker end of the codependent system have an empathic Adult Child who ignores the needs of his or her own Inner Child when around others. Instead, they tend to the other person's needs, paying attention to their own Child and taking care of their own needs only when they are alone or sick. The caretaker's Adult Child has great empathy for the other person's feelings and needs, but little for his or her own, while the taker's Adult Child tends to have little empathy for others' feelings and needs. For each to be balanced rather than codependent, they need to develop a loving Adult; the caretaker needs to develop some healthy narcissism and the taker needs to develop empathy for others. Takers are self-oriented and unaware of the other's needs, while caretakers are other-oriented and unaware of their own needs. Developing empathy for others and healthy narcissism for ourselves is one of the results of Inner Bonding.

Chart 2, from *Inner Bonding*, outlines the codependent system.

### Chart 2: Core Shame-Based Belief: I Am Bad/Wrong/Defective

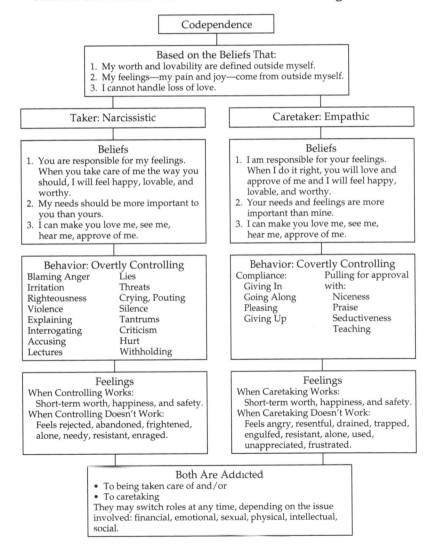

Codependence

**Based on the Beliefs That:**
1. My worth and lovability are defined outside myself.
2. My feelings—my pain and joy—come from outside myself.
3. I cannot handle loss of love.

**Taker: Narcissistic**

Beliefs
1. You are responsible for my feelings. When you take care of me the way you should, I will feel happy, lovable, and worthy.
2. My needs should be more important to you than yours.
3. I can make you love me, see me, hear me, approve of me.

Behavior: Overtly Controlling
| | |
|---|---|
| Blaming Anger | Lies |
| Irritation | Threats |
| Righteousness | Crying, Pouting |
| Violence | Silence |
| Explaining | Tantrums |
| Interrogating | Criticism |
| Accusing | Hurt |
| Lectures | Withholding |

Feelings
When Controlling Works:
  Short-term worth, happiness, and safety.
When Controlling Doesn't Work:
  Feels rejected, abandoned, frightened, alone, needy, resistant, enraged.

**Caretaker: Empathic**

Beliefs
1. I am responsible for your feelings. When I do it right, you will love and approve of me and I will feel happy, lovable, and worthy.
2. Your needs and feelings are more important than mine.
3. I can make you love me, see me, hear me, approve of me.

Behavior: Covertly Controlling
| | |
|---|---|
| Compliance: | Pulling for approval |
| Giving In | with: |
| Going Along | Niceness |
| Pleasing | Praise |
| Giving Up | Seductiveness |
| | Teaching |

Feelings
When Caretaking Works:
  Short-term worth, happiness, and safety.
When Caretaking Doesn't Work:
  Feels angry, resentful, drained, trapped, engulfed, resistant, alone, used, unappreciated, frustrated.

**Both Are Addicted**
- To being taken care of and/or
- To caretaking

They may switch roles at any time, depending on the issue involved: financial, emotional, sexual, physical, intellectual, social.

Both the taker and the caretaker can move into resistance; that is, they can resist what the other wants rather than decide for themselves what they want. Takers are generally resistant to begin with. They tend to set boundaries when boundaries are not needed; they automatically say no before even thinking about whether they would like to do what the other wants. Caretakers may start out by giving in, but will often shift into resistance when they end up feeling unappreciated.

What are your false beliefs about resistance? Check off the items that apply to your Adult Child.

❑ Resisting control is essential to my integrity.

❑ Resisting control establishes my independent identity.

❑ My only choices when another person is attempting to control me are to comply or to resist.

❑ I am really being my own person when I resist.

❑ It's the controlling person's fault that I resist.

❑ I can avoid being controlled by resisting.

❑ If I didn't resist, I would be swallowed up.

§ I resist another's control by:

❑ Doing nothing.

❑ Saying I'll do what he or she wants and then not doing it.

❑ Doing the opposite of what he or she wants.

❑ Explaining, defending, or getting mad about why I shouldn't do it.

❑ Getting critical and making the other person wrong for asking.

❑ Saying I'll do it and then doing something else.

❑ Saying I'll do it and then forgetting or failing to show up.

❑ Procrastinating.

❑ Acting helpless or incompetent.

❑ Becoming apathetic, having no enthusiasm.

❑ Getting sick.

❑ Misunderstanding.

❏ Doing what the other person wants, but doing it halfway.

❏ Doing it wrong on purpose.

❏ Finding some way to sabotage the situation.

❏ Pretending not to hear.

❏ Being uninterested.

❏ Being closed to learning.

❏ Refusing to make a commitment.

§ Sometimes I resist others' control by shutting them out. I shut people out with:

❏ Work

❏ Drugs or alcohol

❏ Hobbies

❏ Illness

❏ Meditation

❏ Spending money

❏ TV

❏ Children

❏ Food

❏ Depression

❏ Reporting, storytelling

❏ Worrying

❏ Reading

❏ Sports

❏ Friends

❏ Sleep

❏ Fantasizing, daydreaming

❏ Silent angry withdrawal

❏ Headphones

❏ Busyness

(add your own)

❏

❏

The problem with resistance is that resistant people are unwittingly being controlled. Instead of making up their own minds about what they want to do, they just resist what the other person wants.

---

**Situations That Often Result in Codependent Responses**

In our daily life we encounter many situations that elicit our typical codependent response. That is, our Adult Child is in charge and either leaves the Child for someone else to caretake or leaves the Child to caretake another's Adult Child. How do you generally respond to the following situations, or how do you think you would respond if you ever found yourself in these situations?

§ Your partner in your primary relationship is angry, shaming, or withdrawn from you.

_____

_____

_____

_____

§ Your boss yells at you.

_____

_____

_____

_____

❧ You receive a traffic ticket.

_____

_____

_____

_____

❧ You are short of money.

_____

_____

_____

_____

❧ Someone close to you has just succeeded at something and you have just failed at something.

_____

_____

_____

_____

❧ Your children are angry at you.

_____

_____

_____

_____

❧ Your children are doing poorly in school.

_____

_____

_____

_____

§ Your parents or siblings have betrayed you in some way—telling members of the family things you told them not to tell, letting you down in some way.

_____

_____

_____

_____

§ Your employee, who is usually very competent, makes a fairly big mistake.

_____

_____

_____

_____

§ Your best friend makes a pass at your mate.

_____

_____

_____

_____

§ You lose a game or a bet.

_____

_____

_____

_____

§ You find out you were completely wrong about something when you were sure you were right.

_____

_____

_____

_____

§ You find out your mate is having an affair.

_____

_____

_____

_____

§ Your partner wants to make love and you don't feel like it but you know he or she will be angry if you say no.

_____

_____

_____

_____

§ Your parents want you to come to a family event and you don't want to.

_____

_____

_____

_____

§ A friend or family member who is generally unreliable asks to
borrow money from you.

_____

_____

_____

_____

§ (For women only) You've been home with your children through their
young years and now you want to go back to school or work and your
husband doesn't want you to.

_____

_____

_____

_____

§ Your mate decides to end the relationship and it's not what
you want.

_____

_____

_____

_____

By now you may have begun to recognize that you rarely operate as a
true loving Adult, that the Adult Child part of you is often unloving to
your Inner Child, and that the feelings of your Inner Child are the result
of this unloving, codependent behavior. Neither takers nor caretakers
are being loving Adults to their Inner Child. In the next chapter we will
see how this came about.

# FOUR

# Things You Learned from Your Parents

Most of us had parents or other caregivers who were Adult Children. They may have been authoritarian, permissive, or a combination of both. Authoritarian parents exert strong control over their children, with the parent winning and the children losing. Permissive parents are absent, neglectful, or indulgent with their children. Often the children win and the parent loses. Both ways of parenting are from the intent to protect against their own pain. There is no intent to learn about their children's needs and feelings, and no intent to learn about the parent's own Inner Child's needs and feelings.

How were you parented? Since our parents or caregivers were our role models for our own Inner Adult, remembering how we were parented is essential for understanding how we treat ourselves, our own Inner Child.

The following visualization can be read silently to yourself, or you can have someone read it to you. Reading it to soft music can help you relax and remember. Sit in a comfortable chair as you go through this visualization.

### Visualization: How Problems Were Handled When You Were a Child

*Settle comfortably into your chair. . . . If someone is reading to you, close your eyes. . . . Take some deep, relaxing breaths, and as you exhale, let all the tension go. . . . Notice which part of your body is most tight—legs, chest, shoulders, forehead. . . . Breathe into it and just let go. . . . Let your shoulders drop, . . . let your jaw relax, . . . unclench your teeth, . . . let the chair support your body totally, . . . let your body be very relaxed.*

*Go back to a time when you were young. Remember your house, your room, your family, or remember not having a family or a house—living with foster parents or in an orphanage. . . .*

*Do you think your parents or caregivers liked you? Did they think you were a wonderful person, or was there always something wrong with you? Did you often feel that you were not quite good enough? Did you feel you were a bad person?*

*If you lived with your parents, how did they treat each other? Were they open and respectful? Was one angry and the other compliant? Both angry? Did they ignore each other? Did they put each other down, being critical and shaming of each other? Did they blame each other? Did they nag? Was there any violence in your home?*

*How did your parents or other caregivers treat themselves? Did they abuse substances? Alcohol, drugs, food? Did one always put himself or herself aside for the other? Did your mother or other caregiver allow herself to be physically abused? Did either of your parents or other caregivers allow themselves to be emotionally abused? Were one or both always overworked? Did either of them ever play? Did either of them ask for what they wanted? Did either of them take responsibility for their own happiness? Were either of them happy some of the time? Much of the time? Was there laughter in your home?*

*How did your parents or caregivers deal with pain? Did they see it as weak to show pain? Did you ever see either of them cry? Were they victims, or did they take responsibility for their own pain? Were they there for each other when one was in pain? Were they there for you when you were in pain? Was anyone ever there for your pain? Or, did you get the message that they couldn't handle either their own pain or yours?*

*Remember a time when you did something that your parents, grandparents, foster parents, or other caregivers didn't like. Perhaps you broke a toy or ruined something of theirs, did poorly in school, talked back or cried, hit a sibling or another child, or got into some other sort of trouble.*

*How did your parents or caregivers handle it? Were they understanding, caring, open? Were they angry, violent, disapproving, hard, silent, critical, judgmental, shaming, cold, or nagging? How did you feel when they were unloving?*

*When you did something positive—accomplished something, got good grades, were kind to someone, showed a talent for something—how did they respond to you? Were they interested and loving, or did they ignore you? Did they attend important school events, or were they too busy or uninterested? Did you feel important or unimportant to them?*

*Take some deep breaths and allow yourself to become aware of how you treat your Inner Child. Is your Adult Child like either or both of your parents or other caregivers? How does your Inner Child feel when you are shaming, judgmental, or absent?*

*Now take some deep breaths and bring your focus back into the present.*

**Writing Exercise**

Write a letter to your mother or other female caregiver telling her how she was as a parent. This is not a letter you will send. You can write it even if your mother or caregiver is dead or abandoned you at some point in your life. Write from your gut, your feelings, your Inner Child.

_____

_____

_____

_____

_____

_____

_____

_____

_____

_____

_____

_____

_____

_____

_____

_____

_____

_____

_____

_____

_____

Now write a letter to your father or male caregiver telling him how he was as a parent.

_____

_____

_____

_____

_____

_____

_____

_____

_____

_____

_____

_____

_____

_____

_____

_____

_____

_____

_____

_____

_____

_____

_____

_____

_____

Write a letter to a grandparent, sibling, or anyone else who deeply affected your life, telling that person how he or she affected you.

_____

_____

_____

_____

_____

_____

_____

_____

_____

_____

_____

_____

_____

_____

_____

_____

_____

_____

_____

_____

_____

_____

## How Do You Abuse Your Inner Child with Unloving Inner Dialogue?

Before we can learn to be a loving Inner Parent, we must first recognize how our Adult Child is unloving. Hardly a moment goes by when we don't have inner dialogue. Our thinking process is generally a one-way conversation from the Adult Child, though much of the time we aren't aware of it, and even less aware of our unlovingness. Our Adult Child is generally authoritarian and permissive, just as our parents were. We can create inner power struggles when our Adult Child is authoritarian and then becomes resistant, such as telling ourselves to go on a diet and then eating everything in sight. The following exercise will help you to become aware of your Adult Child. Each of us learned our inner dialogue from how our parents and caregivers treated us, each other, and themselves. It is only by becoming aware of this dialogue that we can choose to change it. We cannot change something that we do not know we are doing.

Read through the following lists and check off the items that you hear yourself saying to yourself or feel yourself feeling about yourself. The dialogue may be in feelings or actions rather than words.

Some people, in their inner dialogue, use "I" while others use "you." We have written "you" here, but if you are a person who uses "I," then just change the word in your mind as you read.

### Authoritarian Inner Dialogue

❑ "You don't count."

❑ "You don't deserve to do what you want to do."

❑ "What you want isn't important. What he or she wants is more important."

❑ "Don't make trouble. Don't rock the boat. Just go along."

❑ "Don't hurt him or her; that person can't take it."

❑ "Just give in. It's easier than getting into an argument."

❑ "Just lie. That's better than having him or her yell at you."

❑ "You can't have what you want, so just go along."

❑ "If you don't give in, you'll end up alone."

❏ "It's okay to lose you, but don't lose him or her."

❏ "Just do what's expected of you. What you want doesn't really matter."

❏ "You have to do what he or she wants or there'll be trouble."

❏ "You didn't do it right, again."

❏ "You're bad. You should be ashamed of yourself."

❏ "You're selfish."

❏ "Who do you think you are?"

❏ "Work before play."

❏ "You should . . . " "You shouldn't . . . " "You'd better . . . "

❏ "Don't be so stupid. You're such a jerk."

❏ "You'll never be good enough. You'll never do it right."

❏ "You haven't got what it takes."

❏ "What's the matter with you? I'll give you something to cry about."

❏ "You're ugly."

❏ "Shut up. You don't know what you're talking about."

❏ "It's all your fault."

❏ "You're crazy."

❏ "You can't . . . " "You're not capable."

### Resistant Inner Dialogue

❏ "Don't tell me what to do."

❏ "I don't have to. You can't make me."

❏ "I can't."

❏ "Why bother? Who cares?"

### Permissive, Indulgent Inner Dialogue

❏ "If you wait long enough, someone else will do it for you."

❏ "I don't want to go to work. Let's just go back to sleep."

❏ "One more drink won't hurt. I deserve it."

❏ "I deserve a reward. I'll get a muffin."

❏ "I feel lonely. I'll get a muffin."

❏ "She shouldn't have said that. I'll slap her around and teach her a lesson."

### No inner dialogue (withdrawn Adult Child)

Now answer the following questions:

❧ Who was your primary role model for this unloving inner dialogue? Who does your Adult Child sound like?

_____

_____

_____

_____

_____

_____

_____

❧ How does your Inner Child feel when you treat him or her in these ways?

❏ Shamed

❏ Unimportant

❏ Stupid

❏ Angry

❏ Alone

❏ Afraid

❏ Anxious

❏ Bad

❏ Wrong

❏ Inadequate

❏ Unlovable

❏ Defective, flawed

❏ Powerless, helpless

❏ Guilty

❏ Depressed

❏ Resentful

❏ Empty

❏ Unworthy

## Is Your Inner Dialogue Ever Loving to Your Inner Child?

Hopefully, there are those occasions when you do say loving things to your Inner Child. Check the following inner dialogue that you generally hear yourself or feel yourself say (here we have used "I" but if you use "you," just change it):

### Loving Inner Dialogue

❏ "It's okay. I'll do it better next time."

❏ "I look great!"

❏ "That was really creative!"

❏ "I did a really good job."

❏ "It is okay for me to assert myself."

❏ "What matters to me really *is* important."

❏ "I can."

❏ "I deserve good things."

❏ "I'm not responsible for what he or she feels."

❏ "I don't have to give up or give in."

❏ "There must be a good reason I behaved this way."

❏ "I can be happy no matter what happens."

❏  "I don't have to win; I can just have fun."

❏ "It's okay for my feelings and needs to be important."

❏ "Way to go! That's super!"

❏ "It's okay to risk trying new things."

❏ "It's okay to ask for help."

❏ "I couldn't have known that."

❏ "People really do care about me."

❏ "I am very gentle and caring."

❏ "I am funny and bring people laughter."

❏ "If I am being judged, it must be their issue."

❏ "I don't have to take this personally."

❏ "I'll feel better if I give up_____ (insert favorite addiction) but I won't beat myself up in doing it."

❏ "I'm a lovable person."

❏ "I'm a good person."

How do you think your Inner Child would feel if you consistently had loving inner dialogue? Perhaps you can begin to see that the feelings of your Inner Child are determined by the thoughts of your loving Adult or your Adult Child.

### False Beliefs About the Inner Child or Core Self

The things we heard and learned from our parents, siblings, grandparents, teachers, and caregivers, the way they treated us, and the way we experienced them treating themselves and each other created a set of false beliefs that we carry around with us. It is these false beliefs that cause much of our pain.

Check the things you may have heard or absorbed from your role models, as well as from siblings, friends, TV, or society in general—things that your Adult Child may still believe. These are the things you feel shame about. Attempt to read these from the point of view of your Adult Child. Although your loving Adult may know that they are false beliefs, your Adult Child may believe them to be true.

❑ 1. I'm a basically bad, wrong, defective, or unworthy person.

❑ 2. I'm not good enough.

❑ 3. I'm not lovable.

❑ 4. I'm not adequate.

❑ 5. I don't count, don't matter, am unimportant.

❑ 6. I'm in the way, a bother, too much trouble.

❑ 7. I'm bad, wrong, unworthy, defective, inadequate, unlovable, a bother, unimportant, or not good enough because:

   ❑ I'm too tall.

   ❑ I'm too short.

   ❑ I'm too skinny.

   ❑ I'm too fat.

   ❑ I'm ugly, homely, or unattractive.

   ❑ I'm not intelligent enough, not smart enough.

   ❑ I'm stupid.

   ❑ I'm too intelligent, too smart for my own good.

   ❑ I'm not creative enough.

   ❑ I don't have a good sense of humor.

❏ I don't make enough money.

❏ I'm not the best at my job.

❏ I don't drive a nice car.

❏ I'm a geek, a dork.

❏ Nobody likes me.

❏ I'm shy.

❏ I'm too aggressive.

❏ I'm too selfish.

❏ I'm too intense.

❏ I'm too much, but I'm not sure what I'm too much of.

❏ I'm too different.

❏ I'm weird.

❏ I'm scattered

❏ I make mistakes.

❏ I have physical defects or imperfections.

❏ I have problems.

❏ I cry too easily.

❏ I'm too emotional.

❏ I'm not perfect.

❏ I'm not very talkative.

❏ I don't think quickly enough.

❏ I'm just like my father.

❏ I'm just like my mother.

❏ I can't take care of myself.

❏ I need a man to take care of me.

❏ I need a woman to take care of me.

❏ I can't make decisions.

❏ I'll never amount to anything.

❏ I can't tell jokes well.

❏ I'm too sensitive.

❏ I'm too insensitive.

❏ I'm too serious.

❏ I'm not serious enough.

❏ I think differently than other people.

❏ I'm a loner.

❏ I don't have a partner.

❏ I'm afraid to be alone.

❏ I have fears.

❏ I have phobias.

❏ I'm immature.

❏ I'm not a professional.

❏ I never went to college.

❏ I didn't graduate from high school.

❏ I have a small vocabulary.

❏ I can't do math.

❏ I don't read well.

❏ I have no imagination.

❏ I'm not spiritual enough.

❏ I'm too spiritual.

❏ I can't do anything right.

❏ I was abused as a child.

❏ When bad things happen, it's always my fault.

❏ Bad things always happen to me.

- ❏ I have an eating disorder.
- ❏ I'm an alcoholic.
- ❏ I'm a drug addict.
- ❏ I'm too sexual.
- ❏ I'm a sex addict.
- ❏ I'm not sexual enough.
- ❏ I'm crazy.
- ❏ I'm a phony.
- ❏ I'm righteous and arrogant.
- ❏ I'm depressed.
- ❏ I'm superficial.
- ❏ I'm screwed up.
- ❏ I'm boring.
- ❏ I have no personality.
- ❏ I'm a goody-goody.
- ❏ I'm a man.
- ❏ I'm a woman.
- ❏ I'm gay or bisexual.
- ❏ I'm Black, Hispanic, Asian, Indian, Jewish, or some other minority.

(add your own)

- ❏ _____
- ❏ _____
- ❏ _____

Now go back over the items you checked and write next to each one who this false belief came from, or what experiences led you to draw this conclusion.

### Discovering the Truth About These Beliefs

The truth about our false beliefs comes through us from our Higher Power. Learning the truth about these beliefs is an ongoing process, one that you can go back to over and over.

### Exercise for Learning the Truth

Read through the entire exercise and the example before doing the exercise.

1. Pick one of the false beliefs that you checked.

2. Take some deep breaths and relax your body.

3. Choose the intent to learn.

4. Breathe into your heart; visualize it opening like a camera lens. Imagine a golden-white light above your head, the light of love and truth. Visualize the light coming into your mind, your heart, and your solar plexus, filling you with love and truth.

5. With an open mind and a deep desire to know the truth, ask your Higher Power what the truth is about the belief you picked.

6. Allow the answer to come through you. It may not come right away, but it will come. It may come in a dream, or in a creative moment, or when you are talking to someone.

7. Communicate this truth out loud to your Inner Child, directing the information from your head and heart into your gut.

### Example

Let's suppose that you marked "I'm not intelligent enough," and that you got this belief because you never did well in school and your father was always telling you you were stupid. Because of this, you feel inadequate and unlovable. What might come through from your Higher Power?

"Just because you didn't do well in school doesn't mean you are not intelligent. You have a right-brain form of intelligence, a creative intelligence that often doesn't show up on tests."

"You didn't do well in school because you were fearful and anxious about what was going on in your home. Children do not learn well when they are afraid."

"Your father said many things that were not true."

"Your lovability has nothing to do with your intelligence. You are a sweet and kind person. You are very lovable."

Changing your inner dialogue to reflect the truth of your Higher Power rather than the false beliefs you've carried since childhood will eventually change how you feel about yourself. Your Inner Child will continue to feel unloved and unlovable as long as your inner dialogue reflects your parents' belief system. But you as an Adult have the choice to change that inner dialogue. Since our feelings come from our thoughts, changing our thoughts about ourselves also changes our feelings about ourselves and the world.

# FIVE

# *Who Is My Core Self,*
# *My Natural Inner Child?*

In the preceding two chapters we explored some of the many feelings and behaviors that make up who we are in our protected, disconnected, ego state, our Adult Child state. These feelings and behaviors are not who we *really* are, underneath all our fears and false beliefs. These unloving feelings and behaviors are who we are when we are unloved and abandoned, first by our parents and then by ourselves. Now it's time to discover who we are underneath the person we've learned to be out of fear. It's time to discover our core self, our true Inner Child.

If we *knew,* with certainty, that we are in our core lovable, we would have a much easier time loving ourselves. If our parents had held up an accurate mirror to us, through their loving behavior to us and to themselves, we would know that we are lovable.  If that mirror had said, "You are a child of God, created in God's image with the spark of God within your heart, as we all are, and therefore you are lovable. You are lovable just because you exist. Your lovability is not determined by how you look, how bright you are, how talented you are, or how much money we have. You are created through the love in the universe; you are love, and therefore you are lovable," we would know our lovability in the depths of our beings. But instead we were shamed for being ourselves—for our curiosity, intensity, wants, needs, feelings, sexuality. We were shamed for attempting to make ourselves happy when what we wanted conflicted with what our parents wanted. We were shamed for being who we are.

So we took this lovable core self and put it into hiding. In its place we created a false self—the Adult Child, the ego—that we hoped would get us the love and approval we so desperately needed. We lost our connection to our core self, and therefore to our Higher Self and to God, and became lost souls, desperately trying to find the "right" way to be acceptable.

Accepting that we were born loving and lovable is essential to loving self-parenting. If you believe that you were born bad or evil, that you deserved the shaming and abuse that you may have received as a child "for your own good," then you will have a very hard time loving yourself and taking responsibility for yourself.

If you do believe that you were born bad, it is essential that you challenge this belief. The following exercises may help you challenge this false belief.

§ 1. Spend some time with babies, allowing yourself to experience their sweetness and innocence. We have never seen a baby that appeared to be "bad." Some babies are unhappy, because they are hurting physically or emotionally, but this does not make them bad. They start to do "bad" things only when bad things are done to them. What is your primary experience of babies?

_____

_____

_____

_____

_____

_____

_____

_____

§ 2. Get some pictures of yourself as a small child. Do you see "badness" within you?

_____

_____

_____

_____

_____

_____

_____

_____

What do you see?

_____

_____

_____

_____

_____

_____

_____

_____

_____

§ 3. Talk to people who knew you when you were little. Ask them what you were like as a small child. What did they say?

_____

_____

_____

_____

_____

_____

_____

_____

_____

§ 4. Take some deep breaths and move into a state of relaxation. Visualize yourself in spirit form before entering your body. Who were you in your soul? (If your belief system does not allow for this, then just move on to the next question.)

_____

_____

_____

_____

_____

_____

_____

_____

_____

§ 5. Move deeply into your center and feel that little Child within you, the Child you were when you were born. Were you:

❑ Soft

❑ Cuddly

❑ Sweet

❑ Friendly

❑ Kind

❑ Caring

❑ Loving

❑ Happy

❑ Sad

❑ Lonely

❑ Frightened

❑ Content

❑ Curious

❑ Angry

❑ Deformed

❑ Unhealthy

Do you believe any of these qualities make you inherently unlovable?

_____

_____

_____

_____

_____

_____

_____

If the answer is yes, why?

_____

_____

_____

_____

_____

_____

If the answer is yes, define for yourself what it means to be lovable.

_____

_____

_____

_____

_____

_____

Now define what it means to be unlovable.

_____

_____

_____

_____

_____

_____

Now move into the intent to learn with your Higher Power and ask for the truth about the definition of lovability. What is the answer that comes through you?

_____

_____

_____

_____

_____

_____

_____

Work with the above exercises until you *know,* within the depths of your being, that you were born lovable.

## Personality

We each come into the world with our own special ways of being, with a unique personality, our unique expression of God that is us. If our parents were loving, they valued us for what we were, even if we were different from them. If they were unloving, they shamed us for our unique way of being. Part of the job of our loving Adult is to get to know about and value our special ways of being, the unique ways we are wired up.

What kind of child were you? What kind of Child are you now? Since the Child is an enduring part of us, who you were and who you are now are one and the same. As you check off the following items, tune into yourself as you are now as well as remembering what you were like as a child.

❏ Active, fast-moving

❏ Placid, slow-moving

❏ A people person, likes groups

❏ Likes one-to-one contact with people

❏ Daydreamer

❑ Cautious around people

❑ Cautious about trying new things

❑ Spontaneous

❑ Reserved

❑ Outgoing

❑ Quiet

❑ Shy

❑ Left-brained, analytical, thinks linearly

❑ Right-brained, creative, thinks holistically

❑ Both left- and right-brained

❑ Learns through reading, seeing

❑ Learns through hearing

❑ Learns through doing, movement

❑ Thinks in pictures

❑ Thinks in words

❑ Lighthearted

❑ Serious

❑ Witty

❑ Practical

❑ Down-to-earth

❑ Neat, organized

❑ Messy, disorganized

❑ Smart, in the street sense

❑ Smart, in the intellectual sense

❑ Smart, in the creative sense

❑ Smart, in the sense of intuitive wisdom

❏ Funny, good sense of humor

❏ Intense

❏ Determined

❏ Easygoing

❏ Playful

❏ Sensitive

❏ Innocent

❏ Joyful

❏ Peaceful

There is nothing right or wrong, good or bad, better or worse about the above characteristics—they just are, and they need to be valued by your loving Adult for your Inner Child to have high self-esteem. Some of the characteristics that you have may have been ridiculed in your family, while others that you don't have may have been valued. Your job as a loving Adult is to value and accept who you are without thinking less of yourself. One person having a good sense of humor and another being serious does not make one more lovable or worthy than the other. Learning to truly value the characteristics you checked is part of the process of Inner Bonding.

## Looks

In our society how we look is often attached to our sense of worth and lovability. People who don't measure up to a certain standard of beauty often feel insecure, believing that they are unlovable. People who do measure up to that standard often feel insecure, too, because they perceive that people love them for how they look rather than for who they are. It is important for all of us to value how we look, but not to attach that to our lovability.

§ Check the items that describe your perception of your looks:

❏ Cute

❏ Beautiful

❏ Handsome

❏ Sweet-looking

❏ Pretty

❏ Different-looking

❏ Attractive

❏ Exotic

❏ Earthy

❏ Sturdy

❏ Strong

❏ Robust

❏ Frail

❏ Delicate

❏ Soft

❏ Round

❏ Angular

❏ Firm

❏ Pleasant-looking

❏ Sensual

❏ Burly

❏ Large

❏ Big

❏ Small

❏ Little, petite

❏ Tall

❏ Short

❏ Broad

❏ Slender

❏ Regular-featured

❏ Strong-featured

❏ Interesting-looking

Again, learning to value your unique looks without attaching your worth and lovability to how you look is an important part of Inner Bonding.

## Talents

Some people are born with one or more special talents. Sometimes these talents are valued in the family and sometimes they are not. When a person's whole sense of worth is tied up in his or her talent, this can contribute to codependence. Very talented people are often deeply insecure because they believe that people love them only for their talent, just as beautiful people often believe they are valued only for how they look.

Where do your talents lie? Check off the items on the following list that apply to you.

❏ Sports—coordinated, athletic

❏ Mechanical—can make or fix things

❏ Green thumb—can grow things

❏ Clothing—can design patterns or sew

❏ Cooking, creative cuisine

❏ Crafts—weaving, quilting, needlepoint

❏ Drawing

❏ Painting

❏ Ceramics

❏ Sculpture

❏ Landscape design

❏ Architecture

❏ Furniture design or making

❏ Interior design

- ❏ Jewelry design or making
- ❏ Playing one or more musical instruments
- ❏ Singing
- ❏ Writing music, composing
- ❏ Acting
- ❏ Directing
- ❏ Screenwriting
- ❏ Writing, nonfiction
- ❏ Writing, fiction
- ❏ Writing, poetry
- ❏ Science—creative research
- ❏ Inventing
- ❏ Innovative ideas
- ❏ Public speaking
- ❏ Teaching
- ❏ Psychological insight
- ❏ Psychic
- ❏ Networking
- ❏ Humor
- ❏ Healing
- ❏ Marksmanship
- ❏ Eye-hand coordination

❏ Social interaction

❏ Leadership

❏ Business—creating, running, or fixing

❏ Making money

❏ Parenting

❏ Remembering details (excellent memory)

❏ Sharing warmth, love, and caring

❏ Inspiring others

❏ Helping others

(add your own)

❏

❏

❏

❏

Look over the above personality characteristics, looks, and talents that you checked. Now write a mirroring letter from your loving Adult to your Inner Child, holding up an accurate mirror and describing to your Child who he or she is. Below is a sample letter written by someone in one of our workshops.

### Example of Mirroring Letter to Child

*Little one, you are a precious being. You are sensitive, and I appreciate that. I know that you have a caring heart and that you always feel bad when you realize that someone is hurting.*

*You are very smart. Sometimes I'm just amazed at how smart and wise you are, even though I never tell you how much I appreciate that about you. You have a wisdom that has guided me right whenever I listen to you.*

*I love your sense of humor. Your sense of humor has carried me through many hard times. And I like the way you look, which I'm sure you find hard to believe since I've always criticized the way you look. But you are a cute child and I'm glad you are mine.*

*You are very talented too. I really appreciate your ability to write and to think in creative ways. In fact, I don't know where I would be without you.*

*I like the way you use your body too. You are agile and that feels good to me.*

*Most important of all, I know that you are a good and kind person. I know that when I'm there for you, loving you the way you deserve to be loved, your kindness and goodness come out, and I know that when I'm not there for you, you feel sad and alone. I want you to know that I love you very much, just for being you.*

Now write your own letter to your Child:

_____

_____

_____

_____

_____

_____

_____

_____

_____

_____

_____

_____

_____

_____

_____

_____

_____

_____

_____

_____

_____

_____

_____

_____

_____

Many of us have learned to feel our Child's fullness and joy through activities and experiences. Making sure that we have these activities and experiences is part of being a loving Adult to our Inner Child. Life's wonderful experiences allow us to feel as if we have finally come home to ourselves. They give us a glimpse of what it is like to feel joy. The following exercise will help you identify some of the activities and experiences that give you joy.

§ How do you or would you feel and respond to:

Falling in love?

_____

_____

_____

_____

_____

_____

_____

Getting the promotion you have waited so long for?

_____

_____

_____

_____

_____

_____

_____

Thinking about your next planned vacation?

_____

_____

_____

_____

_____

_____

_____

Participating in your favorite sports or hobbies?

_____

_____

_____

_____

_____

_____

_____

Getting recognition for hard work on the job or at school?

_____

_____

_____

_____

_____

_____

_____

Winning the lottery?

_____

_____

_____

_____

_____

_____

_____

Receiving presents?

_____

_____

_____

_____

_____

_____

_____

Being out in nature?

_____

_____

_____

_____

_____

_____

_____

Listening to your favorite music?

_____

_____

_____

_____

_____

_____

_____

Seeing an art show of your favorite artist?

_____

_____

_____

_____

_____

_____

_____

Participating in our favorite activities when we are connected to our Inner Child is a joyful experience; participating in them when we are disconnected may help us get connected, but when we remain disconnected from our core self, nothing brings us joy.

Have you ever had any of these wonderful feelings just being? Or while doing a mundane task such as washing the dishes? Believe it or not, it is possible to have *our very best feelings* while "being" rather than "doing." Whenever our Adult is truly loving and connected to our Inner Child and to our Higher Power, we can experience joy *no matter what we are doing or not doing.* It is not the activity itself that creates our joy, but rather the connection to our Self and our Higher Power. That connection brings the peace and joy that is our birthright.

# SIX

# *The Adoption Decision:*

## Moving into the Intent to Learn

Imagine that you open your door one morning and find a small child on your doorstep, a child who looks just like you looked as a child. Pinned to the child's shirt is a note, "Please adopt me. I'm yours." You look into the child's eyes and see pain, fear, sadness, or anger. This child has been abandoned in many ways and needs love, your love, to feel lovable and worthwhile.

What are you going to do? Are you going to turn the child away, telling it to go elsewhere for the love and approval it needs? Are you going to tell it that you don't know how to love it, that someone else could do a better job than you? Or are you going to accept the job of learning how to be a loving adult to this child, of healing its wounds from childhood as well as meeting its present needs?

This child is you, your Inner Child, your core self. Its many wounds from childhood can be healed only through your love. You may have handed this Child off to relatives, mates, lovers, friends, therapists, co-workers, bosses, or even to your own children in the hope that they would heal the Child's wounds with their love. But it hasn't worked; the wounds of childhood are still there, still haunting you in all your relationships—or keeping you from having relationships.

We are assuming, since you are going through this workbook, that you have already decided you want the job of loving your Inner Child. Your Child, however, may need to hear your commitment. Therefore, you may want to adopt your Inner Child by reciting a formal pledge.

The first step in adopting your Inner Child is to go to a toy store, or a number of toy stores, and pick out a doll or bear (or any other stuffed animal) that represents your Inner Child. It is very helpful to use a doll or bear when you are dialoguing out loud with your Inner Child. You may encounter some resistance at this point in the adoption process. You may have a judgment that it is embarrassing or silly to talk to a doll or a bear, or even to buy one for yourself, so you may find yourself postponing the trip to the toy store. It does take time to move beyond the self-consciousness of talking to a doll or bear, but after a while it will seem natural to you.

This is an important step in the adoption of your Inner Child. Your doll or bear is an essential part of the dialogue process that we describe in the next chapter, and it is also an indispensable tool for learning to give comfort to yourself. You can actually learn to hold and comfort yourself by holding and comforting your doll or bear.

The next step in adopting your Inner Child is to say the following out loud to your Child, looking directly at your doll or bear:

*My dear little* _____ *, I,* _____ *, adopt*

(Your Child's name)      (Your name)

*you as my Child. I commit to learning what it means to love you. I commit to taking responsibility for your feelings of pain and for learning how to bring you joy. I commit to healing your wounds of the past, and to learning how to let you know you are lovable and worthwhile. You are my responsibility, now and forever.*

## The Intent to Learn

The loving Adult is who we are when we are in the intent to learn with our Inner Child and our Higher Power. If you are to follow through on your commitment to love and heal your Inner Child, you must be able to move into the intent to learn. Without the intent to learn, you cannot dialogue with your Child to learn of your wants, needs, pain, and false beliefs, nor can you dialogue with your Higher Power to learn the truth and the loving behavior.

Two conditions are necessary for the intent to learn. First, you must believe that you have good reasons for feeling and behaving the way you do, and that these reasons are your fears and false beliefs, which came from the wounds you received in childhood. You cannot learn when you are judging and shaming yourself for your feelings and behavior.

Second, you must be open to experiencing your pain. The moment you are unwilling to feel your pain, you will instantly move into the intent to protect. You may need to confront some of the false beliefs about pain, which we will do in chapter 10, in order to be willing to experience your pain.

Sometimes, being open to learning is just a matter of deciding to be open, but at other times our fear, pain, or anger may be so intense that we cannot find our way into the intent to learn. When this is the case, we need a bridge to carry us out of the intent to protect (the Adult Child) and into the intent to learn (the loving Adult).

You will not know which bridges work for you until you try them. Following is a list of activities to try when you feel stuck in your protections:

- Listen to your favorite music.

- Draw, paint, or play an instrument.

- Play with a pet.

- Go for a walk.

- Experience being in nature.

- Exercise.

- Dance.

- Read something your Child enjoys.

- Pray.

- Meditate.

- Light candles and incense along with meditation.

- Read spiritual literature—the Bible, *A Course in Miracles,* or any other spiritual literature that you enjoy.

- Breathe into your heart while visualizing light entering your body (see "Exercise for Learning the Truth" in chapter 4).

- Attend a Twelve-Step meeting.

- Write out your fear, pain, or anger.

- Cry while holding your doll or bear.

- Listen to a relaxation or guided visualization tape.

- Talk to a friend about your feelings.

- See a therapist.

- Take Bach Flower Remedies, which can be found in a health food store. The appropriate remedy can be invaluable in opening you to your loving Adult.

- Go on a cleansing diet. Substances such as sugar, nicotine, alcohol, caffeine, and drugs can cut you off from your loving Adult. So can foods to which you are allergic.

- Release your anger in appropriate ways (see exercise below).

### Exercise for Releasing Anger

1. Looking at your doll or bear, give your Inner Child permission to express anger. Tell your Child you will continue to love it no matter what it says or does in the anger exercise.

2. Now turn your doll or bear around to face out and pull it into your stomach. *Visualize* one of the following people sitting in front of you:

   - Someone with whom you are angry at the moment

   - Your mother

   - Your father

   - A grandparent or other relative

   - Any other caregiver from the past

3. Allow yourself to feel little, becoming the Child within.

4. Allow yourself to yell, scream, rage, call names, pound with fists on a bed, beat a bed or couch with a bat, pillow, or rolled-up towel. Keep releasing the anger at the person you have visualized until there is no more anger.

5. It is often helpful to start with someone you are angry at in the present—your mate, lover, boss, co-worker, business partner, friend,

children—and then move into past anger at your parents or other caregivers. Present anger at others is generally a projection of past anger at parents or other caregivers. *Releasing your anger with that person present is not appropriate, unless you both agree to it. The face-to-face release of anger is generally blaming and manipulative and therefore hurtful to you, the other, and the relationship.*

6. After releasing anger at someone in the present and releasing past anger, visualize your Adult Child and allow yourself as a Child to yell at yourself as an Adult Child. Tell your Adult Child all the ways he or she does not take care of you, does not love you, abuses you with shaming or criticism, or ignores your wants, needs, and feelings. Tell your Adult Child all the ways he or she is like your parents or other caregivers. At the same time, try to witness this with the energy of your loving Adult.

7. Turn your doll or bear around and acknowledge that you heard and understood your Child's anger at you. Reassure your Child that you still love him or her.

Releasing anger in this way often leads to an opening of the heart, allowing us to move into the intent to learn. Once you are open, you can proceed to the dialogue process described in the next chapter.

Releasing anger in this way can also open us to our pain and lead to an exploration of the false beliefs behind the pain. If releasing your anger opens you to your pain, allow yourself to cry while you hold your doll or bear as you would a crying child. As you are crying, visualize yourself as a loving Adult surrounding your Child with loving energy. Let your Child know that he or she is not alone in this pain—you as a loving Adult are here, surrounded by the love of your Higher Power. Let yourself cry as long as you need to, and then move into the dialogue process (chapter 7).

## Becoming the Parent You Always Wanted

You've adopted your Inner Child and committed to becoming a loving Adult. What does that mean? What does it look like? How do you get an image of a loving Adult when you may never have seen one?

Understanding what it means to be a loving Adult is an ongoing, creative process. As new situations arise in our lives, we are challenged to discover, with the help of our Higher Power, what the loving behavior looks like. But right now, this minute, with the help of your Inner Child, you can begin to form a concept of what your Inner Child needs to feel loved.

All of us have within us a longing to be loved in a particular way, and we have wishes concerning our childhood—how we wish our mother and father had loved us. How do you wish your mother had been with you? Write a letter to your birth mother, even if your mother died or gave you up for adoption, even if she put you in a foster home or left you with your father or abandoned you in some other way. If you were adopted, write another letter to your adopted mother. Tell your mother how you wish she had treated you as a child.

_____

_____

_____

_____

_____

_____

_____

_____

_____

_____

_____

_____

_____

_____

_____

_____

_____

_____

Now write a letter to your father—even if he died or abandoned you—and to your adoptive father if you were adopted, telling him how you wish he had treated you.

_____

_____

_____

_____

_____

_____

_____

_____

_____

_____

_____

_____

_____

_____

_____

_____

_____

_____

_____

_____

_____

_____

_____

_____

Now write a letter to your mate or future mate, telling him or her how you want to be loved.

_____

_____

_____

_____

_____

_____

_____

_____

_____

_____

_____

_____

_____

_____

_____

_____

_____

_____

_____

_____

_____

_____

_____

Now, give your Child permission to tell you how he or she wants to be loved by you. Write a letter, from your Child to your Adult, telling your Adult how you want to be loved by your Adult.

_____

_____

_____

_____

_____

_____

_____

_____

_____

_____

_____

_____

_____

_____

_____

_____

_____

_____

_____

_____

_____

_____

_____

As an Adult, it is your job to be both mother and father to your Inner Child, and to give to your Child whatever it is you are seeking to get from a mate. The mother part of you needs to listen to your Child, explore the false beliefs, and give comfort and nurturing; the father part of you needs to take loving action in the world in behalf of your Inner Child. Whether you are a man or a woman, you need to learn to be both mother and father to your Inner Child.

Your Child has told you what it wants from you. As we said earlier, learning to take responsibility for meeting your Child's needs and wants is an ongoing process.

# SEVEN

# *Dialoguing with Your Inner Child*

**D**ialoguing with our Inner Child is a skill that can be learned but it takes practice. As with any skill, the more you practice, the better you become at it. We recommend dialoguing for fifteen minutes each morning and fifteen minutes each evening for at least the first year of practicing Inner Bonding. At some point it becomes a natural part of your way of being, something you do constantly, but at the beginning it takes consistency and commitment.

We recommend dialoguing in the morning to discover any dreams your Child wants to talk about, to find out about things your Child especially wants you to pay attention to that day, and to give your Child some love and reassurance. You can use the evening dialogue to find out how you did that day as a Parent—if there were things you missed or things your Child particularly appreciated. It is again a time to give your Child love and approval.

The dialogue process is especially important anytime you experience an upset—anytime you feel frightened, anxious, hurt, sad, angry, or disappointed. Your Child will begin to feel loved and supported when you allow yourself to become aware of upsetting feelings and attend to them as soon as possible. For example, if your stomach is churning at work, you can adjourn to the rest room to find out what your Child is feeling and how best to take care of him or her. With practice, you will learn to do a quick, on-the-spot dialogue with your Inner Child to find out the problem, decide on the loving behavior, and then take the loving action in your own behalf. The more you do this, the more loved and important your Child feels, and the higher your self-esteem.

## Dialoguing with Your Inner Child and Your Adult Child

When you first start to dialogue, it must be done out loud or in writing. If you try to do it in your head, your old unloving patterns from your Adult Child will creep in before you know it. Dialoguing out loud or in writing allows you to hear or see whether you are actually being loving to your Inner Child. Eventually, with enough practice, you will be able to do it successfully in your head.

Whether you are dialoguing out loud or in writing, it is helpful to have your doll or bear with you. In addition, you can use pictures of yourself as a child and as an adult as you do the dialoguing.

## Written Dialoguing

Read through the instructions for both written and oral dialoguing before attempting to dialogue. Start by asking your Child a question from your loving Adult—the Adult who is in the intent to learn. Your heart is open, you are truly curious about the feelings of your Child, you believe your Child has good reasons for his or her feelings, and you are open to whatever pain comes up. Your energy is a circle between your head, your heart, and your Higher Power. Your Adult, your mind, exists within your head and connects to your Child through the compassion within your heart, while bringing through love and truth from your Higher Power. Write out the question with your dominant hand while looking at your doll or bear. If you are dialoguing at work, you can use a picture, but at home it is preferable to use a doll or bear.

Then pick up your picture, doll, or bear, turn it so it faces out, and pull it into you. Allow yourself to feel little, move your attention into your body, particularly into your gut, which is where your Child lives, and answer the question from your nondominant hand.

Moving back into your Adult, empathically acknowledge the feelings so your Child knows you understand. Reassure your Child that you will continue to love him or her no matter what he or she says. Then ask another question, seeking to discover the beliefs behind the feelings, and the past experiences behind the beliefs. Keep doing this until you have a deep understanding of the feelings of your Child and the beliefs of your Adult Child.

If anger comes up, allow your Child to release it through writing, yelling, or hitting the bed or chair. If pain comes up, allow your Child to grieve the losses of the past while holding the doll or bear. When the pain and grief subside, tell your Child the truth about the false beliefs and decide on the loving behavior. If you get stuck regarding the truth or the loving behavior, move into dialogue with your Higher Power.

### Out-Loud Dialoguing

Holding your doll or bear as you would a child, look at it and ask it a question out loud from your loving Adult. Then turn the doll or bear around facing out and pull it into your stomach. As in the written dialoguing, move your focus into your body, allow yourself to feel little, and speak from your Child, answering the question from your feeling place within.

With both written and oral dialogue, visualize your Adult sitting in front of you or surrounding you with his or her loving energy. Doing this visualization is especially important when you are in pain, so that you do not feel alone with the pain. When we were small children, we were so often alone with our pain. Now, as loving Adults we can take away that aloneness by staying with our Inner Child when we dialogue. We can take the loving and nurturing energy that exists within our heart when we are in a true intent to learn and surround ourselves with it as we allow ourselves to speak or cry from our Child within.

Out-loud dialoguing can also be done without the doll or bear while you are driving in your car, exercising, or taking a walk. Some people find it easier to access their feelings when they are moving. Each person needs to find what works best for him or her.

### Dialogue Questions

The questions you ask your Child and Adult Child when dialoguing vary with the situation. There are three basic life situations to consider:

1. Inner Bonding for our everyday lives;

2. Inner Bonding in conflict with others or in painful or frightening life events; and

3. Inner Bonding with memories and beliefs.

### Questions for Daily Dialoguing with Your Inner Child[1]

Taking the time to tune into what you really want in everyday situations not only can help establish the habit of Inner Bonding, but can lead to your spending your time in more satisfying ways. When you encounter a minor conflict—for example, your Child wants junk food, but your Adult wants healthy food—you can negotiate a resolution that satisfies both.

The following questions can help you learn what you want in any given moment:

• "What do you want to do right now?"

• "What would you like to eat right now?"

• "What color do you feel like wearing?"

• "How do you want to spend this day?"

• "What kind of music do you want to listen to now?"

• "Where would you like to go on vacation?"

• "What kind of exercise do you like?"

• "Are you happy or unhappy with the work we do?"

• "Are you happy or unhappy with our relationships—mate, friends?"

• "What kinds of creative things or hobbies would you like to do?"

• "What are some of the things you've always wanted to do but have never done? Have I kept you from doing them?"

Of course, just getting the information will not help you at all. You then have to take action, which we will discuss in chapter 9.

We do not ask these questions in order to indulge our Inner Child, automatically giving everything the Child wants, any more than a loving parent would do with an actual child. But in finding out what our Child wants and what our Adult wants, we can find ways to satisfy both aspects of ourselves.

---

1. From *Inner Bonding,* by Margaret Paul, HarperSanFrancisco, 1992.

### Questions for Dialoguing with Your Inner Child in Conflict with Others or in Painful Life Situations

Much of the pain in our lives occurs as we relate to other people. These relationships present our greatest challenge in terms of being loving to ourselves.

We are also greatly challenged when painful or frightening life situations occur—illness, the loss of a loved one, the failure of a marriage, the loss of a job, and so on. Once you've recognized your feelings of distress and moved into the intent to learn, you can begin the dialoguing process with one of the following questions:

- "What are you feeling?"

- "I know you're angry and I'd like to hear what that's about."

- "Are you angry at me? It's okay to yell at me."

- "It's truly okay for you to feel this anger, even if it's at me. I won't stop loving you, no matter how angry you feel."

- "Are you feeling shamed right now? What has happened that shamed you? How can I help? Am I shaming you?"

- "It's okay to cry. You can cry as long as you need to. You are not alone; I'm here for you."

- "I know you're feeling anxious (or frightened, hurt, worried, depressed, etc.). Can you tell me more about why you are feeling this way? I will not leave you alone with these feelings."

- "How do you feel about _____?" (Name the person you are in conflict with or the difficult life event.)

- "Have I let you down in some way with this person or situation?"

- "How are you needing me to take care of you right now?"

- "What do you want me to do differently with_____?" (Name the person or event.)

- "I can tell that your feelings are too big for me to handle alone. Be assured that I will get the help we need."

Throughout the day, whenever you become aware of feeling uneasy—tense, scared, angry, numb, hurt, or sad—you can ask your Inner Child questions such as:

- "What is causing these feelings? Am I thinking things that are upsetting you?"

- "How can I help you with these feelings?"

- "What do you need from me?"

- "Am I letting you down or not taking care of you in some way? How?"

- "Have I been ignoring you? Discounting you? Controlling you? Shaming you?"

When your Child does not have the answers, the next step is to dialogue with your Higher Power. Reaching out for help from a friend or a therapist may also be necessary.

It's important to take time during the day to affirm your Inner Child, just as a loving parent does with an actual child. You can reassure your Child with statements such as:

- "I'm here for you. I'm not going away. You are very important to me."

- "You are not alone. I am here with you."

- "I love you, and your happiness is very important to me."

- "You are so smart. Thank you for all this wonderful wisdom."

- "Your creativity amazes me."

- "It's okay to make mistakes. You are lovable even if you make mistakes. You don't have to do things perfectly for me to love you and stay here with you."

- "You don't have to do it 'right.' I will continue to love you no matter what you say, even if you say nothing at all."

### Questions for Dialoguing with Memories and Beliefs

Sometimes, present conflicts or disturbing life events touch off painful feelings or memories from the past. When this occurs, you can use the questions below to dialogue with your Inner Child:

- "Is something happening now that reminds you of something that happened when you were little?"

- "Does this person (in the conflict) remind you of mom, dad, a brother or sister, a grandparent?"

- "Does this situation remind you of a traumatic experience that you had when you were little?"

- "I really want to know everything you remember from the past. Your memories are very important to me, and I want to help you heal your fears or your shame."

- "Do you need me to provide someone to help with this? Do you need to be held while you go through this pain?"

If your child needs to be held and there is no one there to hold you, holding your doll or bear as if it were your own Inner Child can, surprisingly, be very comforting. This is a major reason for having a doll or bear to work with.

### Questions for Exploring False Beliefs

As feelings of fear and shame come up, you can explore the beliefs behind them, the beliefs of your Adult Child. Going back to the lists of beliefs in chapters 3, 4, and 5 can help you explore your beliefs.

- "What are my beliefs about my adequacy and lovability? Do I believe I am defective, flawed, bad?"

- "What are my beliefs about my ability to handle pain, to control others, to be responsible for others? What are my beliefs about the responsibility of others for me? What are my beliefs about my resistance? What are my beliefs about my right to make myself happy?"

- "Where did I get these beliefs? What childhood experiences created these beliefs?"

- "What do I gain by acting as if these beliefs are true? What am I afraid of? What would happen if I stopped believing these things about myself?"

Memories can touch off beliefs and beliefs can touch off memories. As you learn about both through the Inner Bonding process, present painful conflicts and events can turn into healing experiences. The ultimate goal of Inner Bonding, of being a loving Adult for the fear and shame of your Inner Child, is to gain both an inner strength that helps you handle life's difficulties and the personal power necessary to make healthy choices.

### Doing a Written Dialogue with Your Inner Child

§ Holding and looking at your doll or bear, move into the intent to learn.

§ Adult (speaking to your Inner Child): What are you feeling right now?

§ Child (Turning the doll or bear around and letting yourself feel little, answer the question with your nondominant hand.):

_____

_____

_____

_____

_____

_____

_____

_____

_____

_____

§ Adult (Turn doll or bear around and hold as you would a child. Empathically respond, acknowledging your Child's feelings with understanding. Give reassurance regarding your love, and ask another question based on your Child's answer.):

_____

_____

_____

_____

_____

_____

_____

_____

_____

§ Child (Turn doll or bear back around and sink into being little, answering from your gut.):

_____

_____

_____

_____

_____

_____

_____

_____

_____

_____

§ Adult:

_____

_____

_____

_____

_____

_____

_____

_____

_____

_____

_____

_____

§ Child:

_____

_____

_____

_____

_____

_____

_____

_____

_____

Continue the dialogue for as long as you want on a separate sheet of paper or in a journal that you keep just for this purpose. Continue to explore the feelings that surface, and the beliefs behind the feelings. If anger or pain comes up, allow your Child to express these feelings. For firsthand examples of the Inner Bonding process at work, see *Healing Your Aloneness* and *Inner Bonding*.

The next step, after exploring the feelings and false beliefs and allowing your Child to release anger and grief, is to tell your Adult Child the truth about the false beliefs and decide on the loving behavior. The loving Adult, the part of us that is connected to universal love and truth, brings this love and truth through from our Higher Power.

## Dialoguing with Your Higher Self or Higher Power

If you do not believe in a Higher Power that exists outside of yourself, it works just as well to dialogue with the highest part of yourself, your own Higher Self. The information will filter through, whether you conceive of it as coming from outside yourself or from within.

Again, you must be in the intent to learn when asking your Higher Power for guidance in discovering the truth and the loving action, and when asking for help in carrying out the loving action. It is the intent to learn that opens your heart to hearing the voice of your Higher Self or Higher Power. You can ask questions or make statements such as:

- "What is the truth about this belief that is causing me pain?"

- "What actions can I take to confront the validity of this belief?"

- "What does my Child need right now to feel loved by me?"

- "What is the loving behavior toward my Inner Child in this conflict situation with_____?"
  (Name a person.)

- "What is the loving behavior toward my Inner Child in this life situation?"

- "Please help me have the strength and courage to take loving action in my Child's behalf."

- "Thank you for your love and your help."

### Doing a Written Dialogue with Your Higher Power

§ Using the dialogue you just had with your Inner Child, pick out a belief that you would like to challenge or a situation in which you would like to know the loving behavior.

§ Open your heart and reach your focus upward, visualizing a ball of brilliant golden-white light above your head. Create a circle of love between your heart and the light. Surrender yourself, through your intent to learn, to knowing the truth. Allow the answer to come *through* you. Write whatever comes to mind without censoring.

§ Adult: What is the truth about? _____

_____

_____

_____

_____

_____

_____

_____

⑤ What is the loving behavior in this situation?

_____

_____

_____

_____

_____

_____

_____

_____

_____

The more you practice this exercise, the more information will come through you, and you will eventually learn to distinguish between the voice of your loving Adult speaking the truth and the voice of your Adult Child making things up.

It's important to remember that whatever is truly loving toward ourselves is also loving to others. The focus, however, needs to be on what is loving to ourselves, to our own Inner Child. If we focus on what we think is loving to others, we may end up caretaking instead of loving and our Child will get cast aside.

Just as your Child will eventually speak to you if you are faithful in your dialoguing, so will your Higher Power. With practice, you will learn to hear the voice of your Higher Power, even though it is generally quite soft. The challenge comes in choosing to listen to the soft voice of your Higher Power rather than the loud voice of your ego. Remembering that your ego's voice, the voice of your Adult Child, is based on disconnection, fear, and false beliefs can help you remain focused on the voice of your Higher Power, the voice of connection, love, and truth. Our egos constantly try to derail us, but if we stay in touch with the feelings of our Child and with what brings us peace and joy, we can learn to stay on track more of the time.

Discovering the loving behavior may be one of the most profoundly creative processes you will ever experience. It is helpful to see this as a creative process in which you are seeking new answers for old problems, or new answers for new problems. Just as an artist, facing a blank canvas, needs to be open to the creative forces moving through him or her, so you need to be open to new ideas and possibilities concerning what it means to love yourself. Being in this creative process with your Inner Child and your Higher Self or Higher Power can be one of the most enlivening and satisfying experiences in your life.

## Dialogue Subjects

Sometimes you may not know what to talk about with your Child. Usually, if you ask your Child what he or she would like to talk about, your Child will come up with an answer. If this does not occur, however, you may want to use some of the dialogue subjects below. If you find that your Child is unhappy with any of these situations and you can't find the way out, explore the loving behavior with your Higher Power. For many of these situations, it may take many explorations to thoroughly understand the feelings and discover the loving behavior. These exploration have to do with current matters. In chapter 8 we will explore issues of the past.

- If you are married or have a lover, explore your Child's feelings about your mate or lover.

- If you are not in a relationship, explore your Child's feelings about that.

- If you work, explore your Child's feelings about the work you do, or about the amount of time you spend working.

- If you do not work at a paying job, explore your Child's feelings about that.

- If you stay home with children, explore your Child's feelings about that.

- If you have children and are in conflict with one or more of your children, explore your Child's feelings about that.

- Explore your Child's feelings about your parents, whether or not they are still living.

- If you have siblings, explore your Child's feelings about your siblings. How does your Child feel about where you were in the family—oldest, middle, youngest, etc.?

- If you are an only child, explore your Child's feelings about that.

- If you have a boss or manager, explore your Child's feelings about this person.

- If there is someone at work with whom you are in conflict, explore your Child's feelings about the conflict and about the person with whom the conflict exists. How does your Child feel about how you are handling the conflict?

- Explore your Child's feelings about how you handle free time. Do you play enough? Do you have balance in your life?

- Explore your Child's feelings about how you take care of your body regarding food, substances, exercise, rest.

- If you drink or take drugs, explore your Child's feelings about that. Who is in charge of your drinking or taking drugs, your Adult or your Adult Child?

- If you smoke, explore your Child's feelings about that. Who is in charge of your decision to smoke, your Adult or your Adult Child?

- If you have an eating disorder, explore your Child's feelings about that. Who is in charge of what and how much or how little you eat, your Adult or your Adult Child?

- Explore your Child's feelings about your friendships.

- If you are in school, explore your Child's feelings about school.

- Explore your Child's feelings about where you live—the house or apartment you live in, and the city or town you live in.

- If you live with roommates, explore your Child's feelings about that.

- Explore your Child's feelings about how you handle money. Who is in charge of the money, your Adult or your Adult Child?

- Explore your Child's feelings about getting to places on time. Who is in charge of that, your Adult or your Adult Child?

- Explore your Child's feelings about the amount of time alone you have or don't have.

- Explore your Child's feelings about sexuality. If you have a partner, explore your sexual feelings about your partner. Explore your feelings about masturbation. Explore your feelings about your sexual identity. Explore your feelings about the degree of your sexual drive.

- Explore your Child's feelings about political and environmental issues.

- Explore your Child's feelings about how much or how little you sleep.

- Explore your Child's feelings about TV.

- Explore your Child's feelings about religion and spirituality.

- Explore your Child's feelings about abortion.

- Explore your Child's feelings about minority issues and civil rights.

- Explore your Child's feelings about feminism and the women's movement.

- Explore your Child's feelings about the men's movement.

- Explore your Child's feelings about cleanliness and neatness. Who is in charge of whether things are neat or messy, clean or dirty—your Adult or your Adult Child?

- If another driver yells at you while you are driving, explore your Child's feelings about that.

- If a checker at a market or a salesperson in a store is rude to you, explore your Child's feelings about that.

- If you see a parent shaming or hitting a child, explore your Child's feelings about that.

- Explore your Child's feelings about the car you drive.

- Explore your Child's feelings about the clothes and the colors you wear.

- Explore your Child's feelings about the way you have furnished your living environment and your work environment.

If any of these issues lead to an internal conflict, explore how your Adult Child feels about the issue and why your Adult Child and your Inner Child feel differently. Are your Adult Child's attitudes like your parents' beliefs?

For some people, it may take weeks or even months before their Child will talk to them. Your Child will talk to you when he or she trusts that you are in the intent to learn and that you will not go away. It also takes time to know whether it is your Adult Child answering the question or your natural, core self, your Inner Child. With practice, you will learn to differentiate these voices. The voice of the Adult Child always comes from fear—the ego voice—while the Inner Child's voice and the loving Adult's voice come from love—the Higher Self.

# EIGHT

# *Deepening the Process*

**B**ecoming a loving Adult to your Inner Child involves loving parenting in the present *and* reparenting of the past. *Both* are essential aspects of Inner Bonding. If you work on healing the past traumas of the Inner Child but never learn to be a loving Adult in present situations, you perpetuate the old traumas by continuing to be the Parent to your Child that your parents were. If you learn how to handle present situations in loving ways but never delve deeply into old wounds, those old wounds will continue to cause problems in all your relationships.

In the last chapter we introduced you to the dialogue process and offered many present situations as dialogue issues. The issues presented in this chapter are situations from the past.

We have found in our work with our clients that it takes about three months of consistent daily dialoguing before the Inner Child feels safe enough to let you in on his or her memories of childhood. Once the Child feels secure in not being abandoned by the Adult in times of fear and pain, then the door to repressed or dissociated memories opens and the Child slowly lets you in on them. Unless you are deeply programmed through ritual abuse to flood with memories, the memories will come at a speed that you can handle.

Healing of pain occurs when you are willing to feel and release the pain until the charge on that painful incident is gone. It is not enough to know in your head that something happened that was painful. You must also feel and release the physical and emotional pain of the experience.

Sometimes memories will come up first as body feelings, especially memories of physical or sexual abuse. Sometimes memories will come up as flashes, like one frame of a movie, with no feelings attached to them at first. Sometimes they come up in dreams, or if they do come up as actual images, it often feels like a dream, or feels as if you are making it up. Dissociated memories—*those memories of extreme abuse that were disconnected from the time they occurred*—are almost always dreamlike and almost always feel as if they are being made up. Repressed memories— those memories that were shoved into the background some time after they occurred—often feel more real.

Often, present conflicts with a mate, a child, a boss, or a friend touch off our old wounds and we have an opportunity, through an intent to learn with our Inner Child, to explore these old wounds.

How do we know when old wounds are being activated? We know through the experience of our pain or our tendency to protect against our pain. When you are in conflict with an important person in your life, or an important person says or does something that upsets you, how do you generally feel? Check all the feelings that apply.

❑ Anxious, tense

❑ Angry

❑ Hurt

❑ Disappointed

❑ Frightened, scared

❑ Thrown away, abandoned

❑ Controlled, engulfed

❑ Unloved

❑ Unlovable

❑ Empty

❑ Alone

❑ Panicked

❑ Rageful

- ❏ Righteous
- ❏ Wrong
- ❏ Blaming
- ❏ Blamed
- ❏ Victimized
- ❏ Numb
- ❏ Overwhelmed
- ❏ Crazy
- ❏ Devastated
- ❏ Helpless
- ❏ Powerless
- ❏ Immobilized
- ❏ Lost
- ❏ Despairing
- ❏ Suicidal
- ❏ Possessive
- ❏ Competitive
- ❏ Jealous, envious
- ❏ Threatened
- ❏ Vengeful
- ❏ Sad
- ❏ Shamed
- ❏ Humiliated
- ❏ Critical, judgmental
- ❏ Terrified
- ❏ One-down
- ❏ One-up

❏ Needy

❏ Used

❏ Unappreciated

❏ Martyred

❏ Trapped

❏ Resentful

❏ Depressed

❏ Resistant

❏ Rejected

These experiences and feelings are a tip-off, a red flag waving that says there is a good possibility that an old wound is being activated. These feelings may also signify that the Adult has not yet learned how to handle a present situation. Only through dialoguing with your Inner Child will you learn why these experiences and feelings are there.

If these feelings and experiences are the result of old, unhealed wounds, the wounds could be from childhood emotional, physical, or sexual abuse. All our painful, unhealed experiences from the past also have false beliefs attached to them—beliefs that may still be governing our lives today. Some of these beliefs were never true, such as beliefs about our lovability; some of the beliefs may have been true at the time but are no longer true today, such as the belief that we are helpless victims of other people's choices.

Deeper work is best done with a close friend or therapist. As you progress farther into Inner Bonding, you may need a close friend or therapist to be with you as you move through your pain. You were alone with your pain the first time, when you were a child. It is not healing to relive all that old pain alone. We all need someone at times to be with us or to hold us when we are in deep pain. The job of our friend or therapist is not to take away our pain, but just to let us know we are not alone in this pain, to extend loving energy to help us move through it, and to offer us mirroring about our healing process. We can do some of the deep work ourselves, but generally not all of it.

The questions below may help you remember and move into exploring your old unhealed wounds and the beliefs that accompany them. Going back over the false beliefs that you checked in earlier chapters may help you connect these beliefs to your past experiences. You may not be able to answer many of the questions about beliefs the first or second time you go through these questions. It does take time and practice with Inner Bonding to connect our false beliefs with our childhood experiences.

You may want to go through these questions over and over to jog your memory. Each time you go through them, you will go deeper and deeper into memory, once your Inner Child trusts your intent to learn. You may want to take one question at a time, or one question a day, and let it sink in before attempting to answer it. You may want to copy these pages so that you can answer the questions again and again as new information comes up. Doing memory work and healing old wounds is a layering process—like peeling an onion. If you go back through these questions every few months, you may find new and different answers coming up each time.

§ Describe the first bedroom you can remember.

_____

_____

_____

_____

_____

_____

_____

§ Did you ever have your own room or did you always have to share a room? How did you feel about this?

_____

_____

_____

_____

_____

_____

_____

§ Who was your most frequent playmate and what did you play?

_____

_____

_____

_____

_____

_____

_____

§ What was your favorite children's story? Is there anything in that
story that helped to form your life script, anything that relates to your
life now?

_____

_____

_____

_____

_____

_____

_____

_____

_____

§ Who decided how you dressed?

_____

_____

_____

_____

_____

§ If someone other than you decided, how did you feel about that, and what beliefs did you adopt as a result of that?

_____

_____

_____

_____

_____

_____

_____

§ What do you remember about your first day of school?

_____

_____

_____

_____

_____

_____

_____

§ What beliefs did you adopt as a result of your experiences of your first day of school?

_____

_____

_____

_____

_____

_____

_____

❧ How did you do in school? Did you ever get into trouble in school? If so, why?

_____

_____

_____

_____

_____

_____

_____

❧ What beliefs did you adopt as a result of your school experiences?

_____

_____

_____

_____

_____

_____

❧ How did you get along with your classmates? Did you have friends at school or did you feel isolated? Were you part of the "in group" or did you always feel on the outside of things? Were you ever picked on, left out, or made fun of at school?

_____

_____

_____

_____

_____

§ What beliefs did you adopt as a result of your social experiences at
school?

_____

_____

_____

_____

_____

_____

§ What were holidays and celebrations like in your home? Were they fun
or tense? Did you feel obligated to celebrate or buy presents, or did you
enjoy doing so? Were your gifts received with love or with ridicule?

_____

_____

_____

_____

_____

_____

§ What beliefs did you adopt as a result of these experiences?

_____

_____

_____

_____

_____

_____

§ How were you disciplined? Were you ignored? Were you isolated? Did you have privileges taken away? Were you glared at, yelled at, shamed, hit? If you were hit, how were you hit? With a hand, a fist, a belt, a ruler, a coat hanger, a board, a stick?

_____

_____

_____

_____

_____

_____

§ What beliefs did you adopt as a result of this discipline (or lack of discipline)?

_____

_____

_____

_____

_____

_____

§ What were the major areas around which you had conflict with your parents or other caregivers, or where you felt shamed or controlled?

❑ Making messes

❑ Toilet training

❑ Wetting the bed

❑ Bedtime

❑ Brushing teeth

❑ Taking a bath or shower

❑ Breaking things

❑ Masturbation

❑ Making noise

❏ Interrupting

❏ Lying

❏ Talking back

❏ Laughing

❏ Crying

❏ Having your feelings hurt

❏ Getting angry

❏ Cleaning your room

❏ Doing your chores

❏ Fighting with siblings

❏ What or how much you ate, not finishing your food

❏ Losing things

❏ Being sick

❏ Being late

❏ Homework

❏ Grades

❏ What clothes you wore

❏ How your wore your hair

❏ Sexuality

❏ Curfew

❏ The kind of friends you had or lack of friends

❏ Drugs or alcohol

(add your own)

❏

❏

❏

❏

§ Based on what you checked, describe times you remember being punished or shamed. What happened?

_____

_____

_____

_____

_____

_____

_____

_____

§ How did you feel at the time?

_____

_____

_____

_____

_____

_____

_____

§ What beliefs did you adopt?

_____

_____

_____

_____

_____

_____

_____

§ How does this affect you now?

_____

_____

_____

_____

_____

_____

_____

§ Was the discipline arbitrary? Did it seem to come out of nowhere? Were you constantly trying to figure out what you were doing wrong? If so, how do you believe this has affected you?

_____

_____

_____

_____

_____

_____

_____

§ What did your mother or other female caregiver do when she was upset with you?

_____

_____

_____

_____

_____

_____

_____

§ What beliefs did you adopt as a result of how she treated you?

_____

_____

_____

_____

_____

_____

_____

§ What did your father or other male caregiver do when he was upset
with you?

_____

_____

_____

_____

_____

_____

_____

§ What beliefs did you adopt as a result of how he treated you?

_____

_____

_____

_____

_____

_____

_____

§ If you had grandparents around, how did they treat you when they were upset with you?

_____

_____

_____

_____

_____

_____

_____

_____

§ What beliefs did you adopt as a result of how you were treated?

_____

_____

_____

_____

_____

_____

_____

§ If you had siblings around, particularly older siblings, how did they treat you?

_____

_____

_____

_____

_____

_____

_____

§ What beliefs did you adopt as a result of how you were treated?

_____

_____

_____

_____

_____

_____

_____

§ What was dinnertime like in your house? What happened if you didn't finish your meal?

_____

_____

_____

_____

_____

_____

_____

§ What beliefs did you adopt as a result of these experiences?

_____

_____

_____

_____

_____

_____

_____

§ Did your family ever take vacations? If so, what were they like?

_____

_____

_____

_____

_____

_____

_____

§ What were your family's religious practices?

_____

_____

_____

_____

_____

_____

_____

§ How did your religious practices (or lack of them) affect you, and what beliefs did you adopt as a result of them?

_____

_____

_____

_____

_____

_____

_____

§ How did your family or other caregivers deal with sexuality? Were they open, closed, shaming, embarrassed?

_____

_____

_____

_____

_____

_____

_____

§ How has their attitude affected your present sexuality?

_____

_____

_____

_____

_____

_____

_____

_____

§ Did you ever get caught "playing doctor" or in any sex play with yourself or with another child? What happened when you got caught?

_____

_____

_____

_____

_____

_____

§ If you did get caught, what beliefs did you adopt as a result of this?

_____

_____

_____

_____

_____

_____

_____

§ Was one or both of your parents physically or emotionally absent a lot?

_____

_____

_____

_____

_____

_____

_____

§ How do you believe this has affected you, and what beliefs have you adopted as a result of this?

_____

_____

_____

_____

_____

_____

_____

§ Did you ever see your father hit your mother?

_____

_____

_____

§ If yes, what beliefs did you adopt as a result of this?

_____

_____

_____

_____

_____

_____

_____

§ Did you experience your mother having control over your father through yelling, nagging, shaming, illness, crying, withdrawal, or some other controlling behavior?

_____

_____

_____

_____

_____

_____

_____

_____

§ If yes, what beliefs did you adopt as a result of this?

_____

_____

_____

_____

_____

_____

_____

§ Did you experience your father having control over your mother through anger, violence, sarcasm, shaming, silence, or some other controlling behavior?

_____

_____

_____

_____

_____

_____

§ If yes, what beliefs did you adopt as a result of this?

_____

_____

_____

_____

_____

_____

§ Did you have chores to do? What happened if you didn't do them?

_____

_____

_____

_____

_____

_____

_____

§ Did you have a family pet? Whose responsibility was the pet?

_____

_____

_____

_____

_____

_____

§ How did your family or other caregivers handle feelings—their own and yours? Were your feelings heard, respected, ignored, discounted, shamed, superficially fixed with rewards such as TV or food?

_____

_____

_____

_____

_____

_____

§ Did either of your parents make you responsible for their feelings by shaming or blaming you when they were upset?

_____

_____

_____

_____

_____

_____

§ Did either of your parents take responsibility for your feelings through complying, anticipating your needs, caretaking, smothering?

_____

_____

_____

_____

_____

_____

§ What beliefs did you adopt regarding responsibility for feelings as a result of how your parents handled their feelings and your feelings?

_____

_____

_____

_____

_____

_____

§ Where were you in your family? Oldest? Middle? Youngest? Only child?

_____

§ How do you believe this has affected you, and what beliefs have you adopted as a result of this?

_____

_____

_____

_____

_____

_____

_____

§ Were you treated differently from your siblings? If so, how?

_____

_____

_____

_____

_____

_____

_____

§ What beliefs did you adopt as a result of this?

_____

_____

_____

_____

_____

_____

§ If you had a younger sibling, how were you treated after this sibling was born? How do you remember feelings after the birth of your younger sibling?

_____

_____

_____

_____

_____

_____

_____

_____

§ What beliefs did you adopt as a result of this?

_____

_____

_____

_____

_____

_____

_____

_____

§ If you had younger siblings, how did you treat them?

_____

_____

_____

_____

_____

_____

_____

§ What beliefs did you adopt as a result of how you treated your siblings?

_____

_____

_____

_____

_____

_____

_____

_____

§ Who was your mother's favorite child?

_____

_____

§ Who was your father's favorite child?

_____

_____

§ How has this affected you, and what beliefs did you adopt as a result of this?

_____

_____

_____

_____

_____

_____

_____

_____

§ Were you ever compared to your siblings or to other children? If so, how did this affect you, and what beliefs did you adopt as a result of it?

_____

_____

_____

_____

_____

_____

§ Did you have nightmares as a child? If so, what do you remember about them? Were you able to go to a parent when you were afraid at night or were you just alone?

_____

_____

_____

_____

_____

_____

§ Did you wet the bed as a child? If so, how did you feel about it and what beliefs did you adopt as a result of it?

_____

_____

_____

_____

_____

_____

❧ Did you ever have temper tantrums as a child? If so, how were they handled by your parents or other caregivers?

_____

_____

_____

_____

_____

_____

_____

_____

❧ Were you afraid to be separated from your family? If so, write what you remember about this.

_____

_____

_____

_____

_____

_____

_____

❧ What beliefs did you adopt as a result of this?

_____

_____

_____

_____

_____

_____

_____

§ Were either or both of your parents or other caregivers:

❑ An alcoholic

❑ A drug addict

❑ A TV addict

❑ A workaholic

❑ A rageaholic

❑ A food addict (had an eating disorder)

❑ A gambler

❑ Mentally ill

§ How do you believe this has affected you, and what beliefs have you adopted as a result of this?

_____

_____

_____

_____

_____

_____

_____

§ Were you adopted?

_____

§ How do you believe this has affected you, and what beliefs have you adopted as a result of this?

_____

_____

_____

_____

§ Were you raised by a single parent?

_____

If the answer is yes, was it because your parents divorced? _____

Was it because your parents never married? _____

Was it because one of your parents died? _____

Was it because one of your parents committed suicide? _____

Were you abandoned by one of your parents? _____

§ How do you believe this has affected you, and what beliefs have you adopted as a result of this?

_____

_____

_____

_____

_____

_____

_____

§ Were you raised in an orphanage? _____

§ Were you raised by foster parents? _____

§ Were you raised by a grandparent or other relative? _____

§ How do you believe this has affected you, and what beliefs have you

adopted as a result of this?

_____

_____

_____

_____

_____

§ Did you ever suffer from severe neglect—being left alone to cry for hours, not being fed, not being held or cuddled, left alone with illness, having illness discounted?

_____

_____

_____

§ How do you believe this has affected you, and what beliefs have you adopted as a result of this?

_____

_____

_____

§ Did you grow up in a very poor family where there wasn't enough to eat?

_____

_____

_____

§ How do you believe this has affected you, and what beliefs have you adopted as a result of this?

_____

_____

_____

§ Did you ever suffer severe physical injury at the hands of one or both of your parents?

_____

_____

_____

§ How do you believe this has affected you, and what beliefs have you adopted as a result of this?

_____

_____

_____

_____

_____

_____

_____

_____

_____

_____

_____

_____

_____

_____

_____

§ Were you overtly sexually abused? If so, how old were you, and who abused you?

_____

_____

_____

_____

_____

_____

These are sometimes the hardest memories to retrieve because they are the most violating, and are therefore often dissociated or repressed. If you have vague memories of sexual abuse or a sense of having been sexually abused, going into therapy and reading books on sexual abuse, such as *The Courage to Heal* by Ellen Bass and Laura Davis, can help you retrieve memories. Healing the wounds from sexual abuse, as well as from severe physical and emotional abuse, is a therapeutic process and generally requires professional help, along with the Inner Bonding that you do on your own.

§ If you were overtly sexually abused, how do you believe this has affected you, and what beliefs have you adopted as a result of this?

_____

_____

_____

_____

_____

_____

_____

_____

_____

_____

§ Did you experience covert sexual abuse—sexual energy, seductive energy, dirty jokes, comments on your body, exhibitionism, or voyeurism— from any family members?

_____

_____

_____

§ How do you believe this has affected you, and what beliefs did you adopt as a result of this?

_____

_____

_____

_____

_____

_____

_____

_____

_____

_____

## Grieving

As deep memories of pain, loss, and abuse come up, it is essential to allow your Inner Child time to grieve. Unhealed wounds are unhealed because unreleased feelings are locked inside. An infected physical wound needs to be opened and drained before it can heal, and the same is true of emotional wounds. The opening of emotional wounds is in remembering them, and the draining of the infection is in allowing the feelings to release through the body's natural way of releasing pain—crying, sobbing, wailing. Grieving is part of the third step of Inner Bonding—a natural outcome of going deeper into the dialogue process.

As feelings come up through the Inner Bonding process, hold your doll or bear, reassuring your Child that you will still love him or her even if you sob deeply. If the pain is too intense, you will need to seek the help of a friend or therapist to be with you while you move through the pain.

## Bringing in the Truth

The fourth step—bringing in the truth from your Higher Power through your loving Adult—is also an essential part of healing old wounds. As long as you operate from your false beliefs, you will continue to perpetuate your woundedness.

The time to bring in the truth about false beliefs is when you are not in a state of grief—when the grief about a particular experience has been released for the moment and you are in a calm state. Grief, like memories, comes in layers, so old grief may come up again and again, but like the tides, it comes and goes. When it is receding and you feel calmer, reach up to your Higher Power and ask what the truth is about the false beliefs that are connected to the memory you were grieving.

You will need to do this again and again, each time the pain comes up. Changing old belief systems takes time. Your Adult will need to tell your Child the truth many times, as well as take new loving action based on the truth. Through repetition of this process, your Inner Child will eventually believe you.

## An Example of This Process at Work

Below is an example of moving through the six steps of Inner Bonding, taking a present issue and allowing it to connect with a childhood issue.

My mate or boss or someone close to me has yelled at me.

Step 1: I tune into feeling *anxious, wrong, and scared.*

Step 2: I move into my loving Adult with an *intent to learn* about these feelings.

Step 3: I ask my Child questions about the feelings, such as:
*"Is there something about this situation that reminds you of something in the past?"*
My Child answers, *"Yeah, it reminds me a lot of what went on at home."*

I then ask, *"What happened at home? How did Mom and Dad treat you when they were upset with you?"*
My Child answers, *"My mother would yell at me and shame me and then tell me that my father would deal with me when he got home. When my father got home he would hit me with a belt."*

As part of Step 3, I move into exploring my beliefs:

I ask my Adult Child, *"What do you think this says about you?"*

My Adult Child answers, *"That I'm bad, and that things are always my fault. That if I could just be good and learn to do things right, people would love me and wouldn't yell at me."*

As part of Step 3, I allow my Child to grieve these feelings. I may cry, sob, hit the bed or a chair with a pillow or rolled-up towel. I hold my doll or bear, visualizing myself as a loving Adult surrounding myself as a Child as I move through the pain. I may release anger at my mate or boss or whoever yelled at me, then at my parents, and finally at my Adult for not protecting me. I may cry deeply for all the times I have felt alone and shamed. When my Child is finished releasing feelings, I reassure my Child. I might say:

*"You are very lovable and I will always be here to help you and take care of you and love you."*

Step 4: When I am calm, I move into an intent to learn with my Higher Power. I tell my Child the truth about the false beliefs and decide on the loving behavior.

First I tell my Child the truth:

*My sweet little one, the truth is that you are good and loving, and that your parents punished you because they did not know how to love you or love themselves. There was nothing you could do to get their love. You could have been the most wonderful child in the world and they still would have yelled at you and hit you because they were yelled at and hit and they didn't know any other way to deal with their feelings. And the same is true now with* _____ _____ *(name of person who has yelled at you). We have no control over how another person treats us.*

I then tell my Child the loving behavior:

*The loving behavior in this situation is for me to tell people who yell at you that I am no longer available to be yelled at, that I will talk with them only when they are open to learning with me.*

I then ask my Child how he or she feels. If there is peace inside, then I am finished with the exploration. If I am still upset, then I will continue to explore until I feel peaceful.

Step 5: The next time someone yells at me, I follow through with the loving behavior and tell that person that I am unavailable to being treated this way. I may go back to the person who originally yelled at me and tell him or her that I'm no longer available to being yelled at.

Step 6: I evaluate my action. The result is that my Child feels loved by me and important to me.

Sometimes, present situations do not touch off past issues and are fairly easy to handle. But when we experience the feelings listed at the beginning of this chapter, it is important to go back to our past and learn the root of those feelings. Moving through these six steps whenever we are feeling bad can bring about the healing of our old wounds.

# NINE

# *Taking Loving Action*

**W**e've now taken you through the first four steps of Inner Bonding:

1. Becoming aware of your Inner Child's feelings.

2. Moving into the loving Adult, the intent to learn.

3. Dialoguing with your Inner Child—discovering the experiences and false beliefs behind the feelings, and grieving the past.

4. Dialoguing with your Higher Power—discovering the truth and the loving behavior.

There will be no actual change in your life, however, until you experience the fifth step—taking loving action. Many people spend years in therapy becoming aware of their feelings and learning about why they feel the way they do, but without loving action in behalf of the Inner Child, these insights and expressions of feelings make no difference to their self-esteem and quality of life. Your Inner Child will not feel important, loved, and lovable until you are willing to take action in his or her behalf. There can be no true healing without loving action on the part of the Adult.

In some ways, taking loving action is the most challenging step of all, because it brings us face to face with the things we may fear the most— the possibility of rejection and aloneness.

What does it mean to take loving action?

The first thing it means is following through on regular dialoguing. You will not know what actions to take to bring your Child joy or relieve pain unless you know what your Child wants each day.

The second thing it means is to dialogue as soon as possible when you are feeling stressed, anxious, scared, hurt, disappointed, or have any other distressing feelings. Your Child will not feel loved and important unless you become aware of these feelings, find out what is causing them, and then do something to relieve them.

The third thing it means is to take the needed action to bring joy or relieve pain. Here is where the real challenge comes in, because those around you may be threatened and angry by the things you decide you need to do to bring yourself joy or relieve pain. Ironically, taking care of yourself—with no intent to harm anyone else—often brings about accusations of selfishness, self-centeredness, or uncaring behavior, especially if you have been on the caretaking end of the codependent system.

When an unhappy relationship, a job you hate, or another major life situation is causing you pain, changing how you respond to that situation or actually leaving can be very frightening. The loving behavior toward our Inner Child is sometimes the hardest thing for us to do, not only in conflicts with others but also in conflicts with ourselves.

## Taking Loving Action in Conflicts with Others

Near the end of chapter 3, we listed some conflict situations and asked you to write down how you usually respond in those circumstances. Now we'd like you to take the same circumstances and, if they apply to you or have at some time applied to you, dialogue with your Higher Power and write down what might be the loving behavior toward your Inner Child in these situations. Even if they don't apply to you, you might want to write down what you think the loving action would be if you ever were in this situation. If you get completely stuck, you can peek at some of the answers we have written following this section.

§ Your partner in your primary relationship is angry, shaming, or withdrawn from you.

_____

_____

_____

_____

_____

_____

§ Your boss yells at you.

_____

_____

_____

_____

_____

_____

§ You receive a traffic ticket.

_____

_____

_____

_____

_____

_____

§ Someone close to you has just succeeded at something and you have just failed at something.

_____

_____

_____

_____

_____

_____

_____

§ Your children are angry at you.

_____

_____

_____

_____

_____

_____

§ Your children are doing poorly in school.

_____

_____

_____

_____

_____

_____

§ Your parents or siblings have betrayed you in some way—telling members of the family things you told them not to tell, letting you down in some way.

_____

_____

_____

_____

_____

_____

_____

§ Your employee, who is usually very competent, makes a fairly big mistake.

_____

_____

_____

_____

_____

_____

_____

§ Your best friend makes a pass at your mate.

_____

_____

_____

_____

_____

_____

§ You lose a game or a bet.

_____

_____

_____

_____

_____

_____

_____

§ You find out you were completely wrong about something when you were sure you were right.

_____

_____

_____

_____

_____

_____

_____

§ You find out your mate is having an affair.

_____

_____

_____

_____

_____

_____

_____

   ❧ Your partner wants to make love and you don't feel like it, but you
know he or she will be hurt or angry if you say no.

_____

_____

_____

_____

_____

_____

   ❧ Your parents want you to come to a family event and you don't want
to go.

_____

_____

_____

_____

_____

_____

   ❧ A friend or family member who is generally unreliable asks to borrow
money from you.

_____

_____

_____

_____

_____

_____

§ (For women only) You've been home with your children through their young years and now you want to go back to school or work and your husband doesn't want you to.

_____

_____

_____

_____

_____

_____

_____

§ Your mate decides to end the relationship and it's not what you want.

_____

_____

_____

_____

_____

_____

_____

Now we will take these situations and give some possible answers to each one. As we said earlier, coming up with the loving behavior is a profoundly creative process, and there is never just one right answer.

Your partner in your primary relationship is angry, shaming, or withdrawn from you:

_If my partner is angry or shaming toward me, I can set a boundary by saying, "I'm not available to being blamed and shamed. When you are open to learning, then let's talk," and walk away. If my partner is withdrawn, I can dialogue with my Inner Child and find out what my Child needs from me to feel peaceful—call a friend and go play, read a book, exercise, and so on. Also, I can let my Child know that I am not responsible for my partner's feelings, and that I still love my Child, regardless of what my partner is saying. I can help my_

*Child to not take my partner's behavior personally, letting my Child know that my partner's behavior is his or her choice—that I didn't cause it and I can't control it. I can explore my Child's feelings, learning about past experiences and resulting false beliefs from childhood that are creating my Child's feelings today. I can allow my Child to release any pain or anger in appropriate ways, by crying or hitting the bed with a pillow, rather than indulging my Child in dumping his or her pain or anger on my partner.*

Your boss yells at you:

*I can set a boundary by telling my boss that I don't like being yelled at, but that I am available, with an intent to learn, to talk over whatever the problem is. I can let my Child know that my boss's yelling does not mean I am a bad person. I can explore what my boss's behavior may be touching off from the past— whether my boss reminds me of my parents, and the beliefs I have about that. If my boss continues to be abusive even after I have repeatedly set firm boundaries, I may have to consider changing jobs, if that is possible. If that does not seem possible, then I have to keep reassuring my Child that my boss's behavior has nothing to do with my worth or lovability, and continue exploring what from the past is being activated by my boss's behavior. I can allow my Child to release feelings of anger and hurt in appropriate ways, not indulging my Child in dumping these feelings on my partner, children, or pets.*

You receive a traffic ticket:

*I can let my Child know that making a mistake does not make me a bad person, and that I, the Adult, am responsible for driving. I can let my Child know that getting a ticket does not take away from my worth as a person. I can explore any feelings in the present that may be touching off old feelings from the past, attaching present feelings to past experiences and resulting beliefs. I can let my Child release anger at the policeman in appropriate ways (screaming in the car after the policeman is gone, or hitting the bed with a pillow when I get home), while letting my Child know that it is not the policeman's fault that I got a ticket. I can also let my Child get angry at me for not being more careful.*

Someone close to you has just succeeded at something and you have just failed at something:

*I can explore my Child's beliefs about failure, examining where they come from in the past, and allow my Child to release feelings of pain and anger in appropriate ways. I can bring in the truth—that failure is a part of learning and does not take away from my worth. I can open myself to learning from the other person concerning how he or she succeeded. I can reassure my Child that I still love him or her, and offer congratulations and support to the person who has succeeded. In offering my love to the other instead of my anger or envy, I feel lovable.*

Your children are angry at you:

*If my children are young, I can assume that they have good reasons for being angry at me and open myself to learning with them, listening empathically to their feelings until I fully understand, while not allowing them to abuse me with their anger. I can then take some action to remedy the situation. If my children are older, I can let them know that I am not available to being blamed but that I am open to learning with them.*

Your children are doing poorly in school:

*First, I can reassure my Child that my children's performance does not say anything about my worth as a person. Then I can assume that my children have good reasons for doing poorly—reasons that may have to do with things at home, things at school, learning disabilities, or health problems—and be open to learning with my children to explore their reasons. I can then take the appropriate action to remedy the situation. If my Inner Child fears being judged by others, I can explore these fears, attaching them to past experiences and beliefs, and bring in the truth. If my Inner Child is angry at my children, I can let my Child release this anger in appropriate ways, making sure that my children do not hear me.*

Your parents or siblings have betrayed you in some way—telling members of the family things you told them not to tell, letting you down in some way:

*I can tell my Child that their behavior is not caused by me and says nothing about my worth or lovability. I can explore old feelings this may touch off in me from the past, releasing the pain from both past and present. I can then be open to learning with them about why they made the choices they made. I can make sure that in the future I do not put myself in that position.*

Your employee, who is usually very competent, makes a fairly big mistake:

*I can be open to learning about what may be going on with my employee and find out if the problem is personal or work-related. If it is work-related, we can explore ways to remedy the situation. If it is personal, I can offer support for my employee getting whatever help he or she needs to deal with the situation.*

Your best friend makes a pass at your mate:

*First, I can explore my Inner Child's feelings of betrayal, assessing whether old issues are being activated and allowing my Child to release anger and hurt in appropriate ways. Then, I can be open to learning with both my friend and my mate and attempt to understand why this would occur. I can decide whether I want to remain friends with this person, and if I decide I do want to retain the friendship, I can set appropriate boundaries with my friend. I can explore with my mate how he or she feels about this situation.*

You lose a game or a bet:

*If my Child is feeling bad, I can explore these feelings and discover what past experiences and false beliefs create these bad feelings. I can reassure my Child that his or her worth and lovability is not dependent on winning—that I will go on loving my Child no matter whether he or she wins or loses. I can let my Child know about the many things I value about him or her that have nothing to do with winning or losing games or bets.*

You find out you were completely wrong about something when you were sure you were right:

*I can explore my Child's beliefs about being wrong. Does my Child believe that being wrong means he or she is bad, unworthy, or unlovable? If so, why? What past experiences created this false belief? I can let my Child know the truth—that being wrong about something or making a mistake has nothing to do with worth or lovability, and that I will continue to love him or her. I can help to free my Child by giving him or her permission to be wrong. I can acknowledge to the other person that I was wrong, and even laugh about it, rather than blaming myself for it.*

You find out your mate is having an affair:

*I can be there for my Child's feelings of hurt, betrayal, and abandonment, and give my Child an appropriate arena to release the pain and anger, or even the rage that may come up. I can explore whether this situation activates past experiences of abandonment and betrayal that may have occurred in my family. I can reassure my Child that my mate's choices have nothing to do with my worth and lovability. When I have released the hurt and anger and have reached a place of true openness and can be in an intent to learn, I can explore with my mate his or her reasons for making that choice. Does it have anything to do with me personally or with things lacking in our relationship, or does it have to do only with something going on with my mate? In either case, I can continue to learn about myself and my mate. At some point, I will need to explore with my*

*Child whether I can best take care of him or her by staying in the relationship or by leaving.*

Your partner wants to make love and you don't feel like it, but you know he or she will be hurt or angry if you say no:

*I can let my Child know that he or she had good reasons for not wanting to make love and that I am not responsible for my partner's feelings. I can be open to learning about my own feelings and reasons, and explore with my partner if he or she is open. If my partner remains closed, I can ask my Child what he or she wants from me to feel okay. Do we need to leave and go into another room? Do we need to just go to sleep? Do we need to do something else like read a book? Do we need to do more dialoguing? I can keep reassuring my Child that he or she has the right to say no, that my body belongs to me and not to my partner, and that my partner is responsible for his or her own feelings.*

Your parents want you to come to a family event and you don't want to go:

*I can let my Child know that he or she has the right and the freedom to say no, that we are not obligated to do something just because someone else wants us to. When I speak to my parents about it, I can put my Child behind me so that only my Adult is handling the situation, and I can clearly state that I don't want to go. If my parents are shaming, I can set a boundary by saying, "I am not available to be shamed for my decision." If my parents persist in shaming me, I can hang up the phone or walk away from the conversation. If my parents want to know why from a true intent to learn, then I can tell them the reason, having first discovered it with my Child.*

A friend or family member who is generally unreliable asks to borrow money from you:

*I can let my Child know that he or she is under no obligation to lend money to anyone—that I have the right to say no. Then I can put my Child behind me and have my Adult handle the situation, stating firmly that I am unwilling to lend this person money. If the person becomes abusive, I can immediately end the conversation. If the person wants to know why, I can tell the truth about how I feel about lending money in general or how I feel about lending money to this particular person.*

(For women only) You've been home with your children through their young years and now you want to go back to school or work and your husband doesn't want you to:

*If my husband is shaming me for what I want, telling me I am selfish, I can set a boundary by saying that I am not available to be shamed and will talk with him about it only when he is open to learning and caring about me. I can let my Child know that I have the right to want what I want, even if my husband is upset, and that he is responsible for his own feelings. I can work with my Child's false beliefs that my husband's feelings are her responsibility and that she is selfish if she does what she wants, until both my Adult Child and my Child know that I have the right to work or learn or do whatever else makes me happy. Then I can go and do it and continue to set boundaries concerning being shamed and blamed. I can also let my Child know that I will take care of her if my husband decides to leave me. If I believe this is a possibility, I can explore my fears of being alone. If my Child is afraid I cannot take care of her emotionally, then continued work with Inner Bonding will eventually resolve this fear. If my Child is afraid I cannot take care of her or the children financially, and if this is a realistic fear, then I will need to do some groundwork in this area before I can feel the freedom to truly take care of myself and do what I want to do.*

Your mate decides to end the relationship and it's not what you want:

*I can give my Child an arena, either alone or with a therapist, to release anger, hurt, and grief. I can let my Child know in many ways that he or she is worthy and lovable even if my mate doesn't want the relationship. I can let my Child know that I will take care of him or her. When I can be open to learning with my mate, I can explore the reasons he or she no longer wants the relationship and what my part has been in bringing about the end of the relationship. I can use this difficult situation to learn more about myself so that I don't create the same system in my next relationship.*

Showing up for our Inner Child in conflict with others means:

1. Putting our Child behind us and dealing with the conflict from our Adult.

2. Moving into the intent to learn with ourselves and the other.

3. If the other person remains closed, setting appropriate boundaries by leaving the interaction until the other person is open, letting the other person know that we are not available for shame and blame.

4. Exploring with our Inner Child any pain that came up as a result of the conflict.

### Loving Behavior When in Conflict with Oneself

Often the conflict we experience has nothing to do with others. Instead, the conflict may be between our own Adult Child and our own Inner Child. We may be suffering as a result of ignoring or indulging our Inner Child—being a permissive Inner Parent—or from controlling or shaming our Inner Child—being an authoritarian Inner Parent.

With each of the following situations, dialogue with your Higher Power and write down what might be the loving behavior toward your Inner Child. Even if you have never had this inner conflict, you might want to write down what you think the loving action would be if you ever were in this situation. Again, if you get stuck, you can look at some of the answers we have written following this section.

§ You are short of money.

_____

_____

_____

_____

_____

_____

_____

§ You have just decided it is time to lose weight, but you really want to stop on your way home and pick up some muffins.

_____

_____

_____

_____

_____

_____

_____

§ You have decided to get up early and work out, but when the time comes you roll over and go back to sleep. Then, later, you feel upset about it.

_____

_____

_____

_____

_____

_____

_____

§ You have work you need to get done, but what you really want to do is lie down and read a novel.

_____

_____

_____

_____

_____

_____

_____

§ You make very good money at your job but you hate the job.

_____

_____

_____

_____

_____

_____

_____

§ Your Child wants a dog but your Adult or Adult Child doesn't want the responsibility.

_____

_____

_____

_____

_____

_____

§ Your Child wants to learn to play the piano, but your Adult or Adult Child believes you don't have the money to get a piano and take lessons.

_____

_____

_____

_____

_____

_____

§ Your Child wants more time to play and pursue hobbies and other interests, and your Adult Child believes you need to spend your time working and being there for others.

_____

_____

_____

_____

_____

_____

§ Your Child wants some time alone, and your Adult or Adult Child believes you need to spend more time with your family.

_____

_____

_____

_____

_____

_____

_____

§ There is something you really want to buy but can't afford.

_____

_____

_____

_____

_____

_____

_____

Again, we will take these situations and give some possible answers to each. Remember, there is never just one right answer. As you practice Inner Bonding and move deeper and deeper into your process, you will be able to come up with new and creative answers that are uniquely right for you and that work for you.

You are short of money:

_If I am spending too much, I can explore why I am indulging my Child in spending. Does this go back to patterns I learned in my family? Were my parents indulgent spenders with themselves or with me? Or were they the opposite and I'm rebelling against them? I can also take steps to cut down. I can explore ways of earning more money and explore beliefs that may be limiting my earning power. Looking into these beliefs may take me into past feelings and experiences that I can explore. I can ask for other people's advice on how to better handle money. I can reassure my Child that being short of money does not take_ *away from his or her worth or lovability—that taking care of money is the Adult's job, and that I will strive to take better care of my Child. I can allow my Child to release feelings of pain and fear in appropriate ways, and I can allow my Child to release anger at me, the Adult Child, if I have not been taking good care of my Child.*

You have just decided it is time to lose weight, but you really want to stop on your way home and pick up some muffins:

*I can stop the car and dialogue right there with my Inner Child, exploring why he or she feels a need to fill up with a muffin. Is my Child feeling alone? Have I been ignoring my Child? Are there feelings from the day that my Child needs to express and release? Are there ways in which I haven't taken good care of my Child today? Are there old issues that I have been avoiding with food— issues of childhood abuse? Am I using food to stuff down my feelings of fear and aloneness? Am I caught in a resistant and rebellious pattern regarding food? Instead of avoiding the feelings and indulging my Child in filling up with food, I can take responsibility and fill my Child up with my love and the love of my Higher Power.*

You have decided to get up early and work out, but when the time comes you roll over and go back to sleep. Then, later, you feel upset about it:

*I can explore with my Child who really wants to work out—my Adult or my Child? Perhaps both aspects want to exercise but my Adult has chosen a form of exercise that my Child doesn't like. Perhaps my Child would rather play tennis or dance than work with weights. Maybe both aspects really do want to work out but my Adult Child indulges my Child in sleeping, which may not be taking good care of my Child. Perhaps I'm pushing myself too hard and not getting enough sleep. Perhaps I really don't value my Child, and therefore my body, enough to really take good care of it. If not, then this is the area where I need work. By dialoguing with my Child and my Higher Power, I can find the answers to these questions.*

You have work you need to get done, but what you really want to do is lie down and read a novel:

*I can dialogue with my Child and explore whether I have a good balance between work and play. If not, then I have work to do to create a better balance. If I do have a good balance, then am I indulging my Child by not getting the work done? Is my Adult Child procrastinating? Or does my Child really dislike the work I do? If that is the case, then I can do much dialogue concerning the work situation. Perhaps I need to negotiate with my Child and decide when we will work and when we will relax and read, and then follow through on what we have negotiated.*

You make very good money at your job but you hate the job:

*I can explore with my Child other possibilities for work. This may take place over a period of time. I may need to investigate other kinds of work, get some career counseling, or look into going back to school. Perhaps there are ways of making this job better. Perhaps it's not so much the job but my not taking care of my Child on the job. I may need to explore my beliefs and attitudes concerning the work or how I deal with other people at work. I may need to provide more playtime for my Child for the work to be acceptable.*

Your Child wants a dog but your Adult or Adult Child doesn't want the responsibility:

*I can explore with my Child his or her feelings about having a pet, and I can explore my feelings as an Adult about the responsibility. If it truly is too difficult to have a dog, perhaps my Child would accept another pet, one that doesn't need as much attention. Perhaps I need to explore with my Adult Child my feelings about responsibility, about giving to myself.*

Your Child wants to learn to play the piano, but your Adult or Adult Child believes you don't have the money to get a piano and take lessons:

*I can look into renting a piano and perhaps taking lessons in a group. I can even look into using a friend's piano, or starting on a small keyboard, which I may be able to purchase used. I can explore any fears of failure that may be blocking my fulfilling my Child's request. I can explore beliefs I may have about not deserving to have what I want.*

Your Child wants more time to play and pursue hobbies and other interests, and your Adult Child believes you need to spend your time working and being there for others:

*I can explore fears I may have of others being angry at me if I do what I want. I can explore fears I may have that if I let my Child play, he or she will take over and I will never get anything done. I can explore beliefs I have about whether I deserve to have the time to play. Then I can take action to create the time and see what happens.*

Your Child wants some time alone, and your Adult or Adult Child believes you need to spend more time with your family:

*I can dialogue with my Child and explore my beliefs about what I am and am not responsible for, and my beliefs about whether I am being selfish in taking time alone. Do I value my Child enough to make sure my Child gets his or her needs met? Am I afraid my family doesn't love me enough to support what I need? Once I understand my fears and beliefs, I can then take the action of setting aside some time for myself and see what happens.*

There is something you really want to buy but can't afford:

*I can look at where I can cut down on my spending and start a special savings account, into which I put a small amount of money each week or each month, until I have enough to buy the item I want. I can look into other ways of earning money. Once I decide on how to get what I want, I follow through on this decision.*

Obviously, until we are willing to confront our fears and beliefs by taking an action and seeing what happens, we will remain stuck in our unhappiness. We all have many fears and beliefs that keep us stuck in nonaction. The next chapter will help you explore some of these fears and beliefs.

# TEN

# Getting Stuck:
# Facing Your Fears

All of us have numerous blocks to accepting the job of becoming loving Adults—blocks to our intent to learn, blocks to taking personal responsibility for our pain and joy. These barriers are our fears and the false beliefs that create those fears. When we get stuck in our healing process, enmeshed in our ego or Adult Child, we can free ourselves by exploring the fears and false beliefs that create our ego state.

What are your fears about being in the intent to learn with your Inner Child and Higher Power or about taking responsibility for your Inner Child? Check those fears that apply to you

❑ **Fear of your Child's anger at you:**

Are you afraid of hearing your Child's anger at you for not taking better care of him or her?

❑ **Fear of your Child's anger at others:**

Are you afraid, if you start to get to know your Child, of experiencing your Child's anger at others? Are you afraid you will hurt others if you become open to your anger? If you have never taken responsibility for releasing anger in appropriate ways, if you have always dumped it on others, you may be afraid of your rage or violence. It is important to learn that your Adult can place limits on your acting out your anger toward others, as well as create a safe environment for releasing old and present anger and learning from it. There is a big difference between closed and open anger. Closed anger is anger that is acted out and is blaming toward others. It is the anger of a victim, an Adult Child. Open anger is anger that is released in appropriate ways, for example, through screaming and pounding when no one around. It leads to learning and personal responsibility. With open anger, the loving Adult is present and open to learning; with closed anger, the Adult Child is in charge.

❏ **Fear of experiencing your Child's pain:**

Many of us have numerous false beliefs about pain. What are your false beliefs about pain? Check off the ones that apply to you.

❏ I can't handle my pain, especially the pain of disapproval, rejection, or abandonment, the pain of being shut out—the pain of isolation and aloneness.

❏ If I open to my pain, I will fall apart, go crazy, or die.

❏ If I open to my pain, it will be unending.

❏ Once I start to cry, I'll never stop.

❏ Showing pain is a sign of weakness.

❏ People will think less of me if they see me cry. If I cry I will be rejected, or people will think I'm crazy.

❏ No one really wants to hear about my pain.

❏ No one can handle the depth of my pain.

❏ My problems are so trivial compared with those of other people that I have no right to be in pain.

❏ Why should I have to feel this pain? It's not my fault and I shouldn't have to go through it.

❏ There's no point in opening to pain. It doesn't make anything better. "Why cry over spilt milk?"

❏ Why should I dredge up the past? The past is the past and it doesn't affect me now.

When we are in the intent to learn, we are willing to feel our original pain of not being loved as we needed to be loved; we are willing to face the pain of our aloneness. When we are in the intent to protect, we guard against experiencing that original pain, and against the grief we will feel when we let ourselves in on how we weren't loved.

Fear of losing control over the people and events that cause pain, and fear of losing control over the experience of pain, is one of the major blocks to the intent to learn with the Child.

❑ **Fear of finding out the truth about your parents—that you were not loved and maybe never will be loved by your parents:**

If we were unloved by our parents, we had only two choices regarding how we dealt with it: (1) we could decide that it was our fault—that we were bad, unworthy, flawed, unlovable (core shame), or (2) we could realize that our parents were incapable of loving us. If we had seen the truth, that our parents were incapable of loving us and that we would never get the love we needed, we would have felt hopeless. Had we felt overwhelming hopelessness, we might have become sick or had an accident and died. So most of us decided it was our fault, which gave us the hope that if we were good and did things right, we would be loved. We chose shame to protect against the hopelessness and despair of knowing the truth. That was a lifesaving or sanity-saving decision at the time, but now that decision keeps us locked in our shame. To be open to learning and to heal the core shame, we have to accept the truth and grieve it.

❑ **Fear of being controlled and betrayed by your Inner Child:**

Perhaps you, as an Adult Child, are in a power struggle with your Inner Child, fearing that if you open to learning and caring about your Child, he or she will take over and control you. If you experience any of the following inner dialogue, your Adult Child may be resisting your Inner Child. Check off those items that you may have heard yourself say as you went through this workbook.

❑ This process is really dumb.

❑ This theory is simplistic.

❑ I don't buy this Adult-Child junk. What do you think I am, schizophrenic?

❑ I've done all sorts of different therapies and workshops. None of them have worked. Why should this be any different? So why bother? It won't work.

❑ I don't know how to love my Child.

You may have numerous false beliefs about your Child that lead you to believe you will be controlled or betrayed by your Child. What are your beliefs about your Child? Check the ones that apply.

❏ Your Child is a troublemaker, unruly.

❏ Your Child always wants its own way.

❏ Your Child is untrustworthy and will just get you into trouble.

❏ Your Child is lazy and will never allow you to get anything done if you open to learning about him or her.

This may be who your Adult Child is but it is not who your Inner Child is.

❏ **Fear of being responsible for yourself, your own pain, joy, and self-esteem, rather than trying to gain self-esteem through love and approval from others:**

What are your Adult Child's beliefs about what gives you self-esteem, relieves pain, and brings you joy? Check those that apply:

❏ Getting love and approval from as many people as possible is what makes me the happiest.

❏ Getting the love and approval of my mate is what makes me the happiest.

❏ It makes me happier and raises my self-esteem to get love rather than to give it, to be seen rather than to see, to be heard rather than to hear.

❏ Others can make up to me the lack of love I received as a Child, and it is their job to do this. If I am married, it is my mate's job to love me in the way I was never loved by my parents, and when he or she does it right, I will be happy and have high self-esteem.

❏ My pain and low self-esteem are the result of others not loving me the way they should.

❏ My pain and low self-esteem are the result of my mate not loving me the way he or she should.

❏ It's more important to have control over getting other people's love and approval and avoiding their disapproval than it is to give love and approval to myself.

❏ Since I am incapable of taking care of my own Inner Child, it is up to others to do it for me.

❏ No matter how much I love myself and take care of myself, I can never make myself as happy as someone or something else can.

❏ It's not my job to make myself happy. The job belongs to my:

   ❏ Parents

   ❏ Children

   ❏ Mate

   ❏ Future mate

   ❏ Manager, Boss

   ❏ Friends

   ❏ Therapist

   ❏ Minister, Priest, Rabbi

❏ I will have high self-esteem only when I am financially successful.

❏ **Fear that you are incapable of developing a true Adult:**

When the only Adult you are aware of is your Adult Child, when you have never developed a concept of a loving Adult nor seen that role-modeled, you may fear that developing a true Adult is an impossible task. It is a major challenge, but it certainly is not impossible. Because we have free choice regarding our intent, we can always choose to be on the path of learning to be a loving Adult.

❏ **Fear of discovering that your core is bad, wrong, or unworthy:**

If you were shamed as a child for being yourself, you may fear that in opening yourself to learning about your Child, you will discover that you are a bad person. You may fear that because you did some bad things as a child, such as beat up siblings, steal, or set fires, or because you have done bad things as an Adult Child, that your core self is bad. It's important to realize that whatever bad things you have done to hurt others came from being unloved, by your parents as a child and by your Adult Child as an adult, rather than from being unlovable in your core self. Underneath all the angry, hurtful, protective behavior is a lovable

Child, but you will not understand that until you take the chance of getting to know this Child.

❏ **Fear of confronting an inner conflict and knowing the truth:**

Your Child may want things your Adult Child doesn't want and vice versa. Perhaps there are conflicts over the kind of work you do, whether or not you want a family, who you spend time with, whether or not you want your relationship with your mate, where you would like to live. The fear arises because, if you really know how you feel about these things, you may have to do something about them. You can resolve these inner conflicts only through an intent to learn with your Child and your Higher Power. When you allow these conflicts to go on without addressing them, your Child may eventually sabotage you through physical illness or depression.

❏ **Fear of failure at dialoguing:**

Some people fear that they do not have an Inner Child, that they are empty inside. They are afraid that if they try dialoguing, nothing will happen. Other people doubt that they have an Adult and, as stated earlier, fear that they are incapable of developing one. Rather than risk failure, they choose not to try.

❏ **Fear of finding out that everything in your present or past relationships is your fault, that you are the wrong one:**

So often in our relationships we see clearly what the other person is doing to cause the problems. When we open to learning with our Child, we find out what it is we are doing to cause our own unhappiness. It is not helpful, however, to see ourselves as "wrong" or "at fault." Instead, we need to recognize that we are each *responsible* for our end of any interaction. Rather than placing blame, we learn to look at what we can do differently to relieve our pain and bring joy to ourselves.

❏ **Fear of outgrowing a relationship:**

Many people fear that if they open to learning and move toward their wholeness and personal power, and if their mate does not also open, they will no longer want the relationship they are in. This is a realistic possibility and one that must be confronted if you want your wholeness. Would you rather give up you to keep the relationship, or are you willing to risk losing the relationship to find your wholeness and personal power?

❑ **Fear that if you take responsibility for your own happiness, pain, and self-esteem, you will never get the love from another that you want, or will end up alone:**

People often believe that they will get love only if they are needy and dependent, that if they are whole and independent they will end up alone. The truth is that we push people away with our dependency. We have to become independent before we can be interdependent. Interdependence occurs when two whole people share themselves with each other and care about each other without caretaking.

❑ **Fear that if you move into the intent to learn and take care of yourself, you will be seen as selfish. Fear that you do not have the right to take care of yourself.**

Many of us have been taught to believe that taking care of oneself is selfish. The truth is that taking care of ourselves is being personally responsible; we are being selfish when we expect others to take care of us. When people who expect us to caretake them call us selfish for taking care of ourselves, it is our job as a loving Adult to reassure our Child that we are not responsible for other's feelings. It is not only our right to take care of ourselves, it is our responsibility.

❑ **Fear that if you take care of yourself, you won't want or need a relationship:**

In our workshops, people sometimes ask, "If I really take care of myself, why would I want or need a relationship?" The answer is: to share, learn, grow, and offer your love. The more we fill ourselves up from within, the more love we have to offer and the more we want to offer it. When we are empty inside because our Adult is not taking care of our Child, we seek relationships to get love, but when we are full we seek them to offer our love. In addition, we seek spiritual partners to help us continue to grow more and more loving.

## Writing a Letter of Intention

One way of helping yourself get unstuck is to write a letter of intention when you are feeling clear and open. State your intent to learn with and from your Inner Child and your Higher Power. Write down why this is important to you, and how you have benefited from being open to learning. List the things you have done in the past that have opened you when you were protected and stuck in your protections. Write about your commitment to learning to love your Inner Child, and why you value your Child. Then, when you are stuck, refer to your letter of intention. It will remind you why being open to learning and taking responsibility for your Child is important to you.

If you feel open and clear right now, write your letter of intention:

_____

_____

_____

_____

_____

_____

_____

_____

_____

_____

_____

_____

_____

_____

_____

_____

_____

_____

_____

All of us get stuck sometimes. When you feel stuck, review the list of false beliefs in this chapter, look over the ways of moving into an intent to learn listed in chapter 6, call upon your Higher Power for help, and read your letter of intention. At times, it is necessary to seek the help of a therapist, especially if memories of abuse are coming up or if you are involved in a codependent relationship and are having trouble seeing your end of it. Sometimes life situations such as a new baby, a new job, getting fired, children leaving the home, a divorce, moving to a new city, inability to find a partner, or a loved one dying can be too difficult to handle without professional help. It is always beneficial to have an objective person to call on whenever you need help with your healing process. You may need professional help if you are having trouble starting the Inner Bonding process. You may need the safety of a therapist's office to begin learning about your Child.

The bottom line in getting unstuck versus staying stuck in your healing process is: are you willing to move into the intent to learn and face the fear and pain within your Inner Child, or are you unwilling to face this fear and pain? When your highest priority is to be a loving human being to yourself and others, when this is more important than protecting against your fears and pain, you will get unstuck.

We'd like to end this chapter with a visualization that may help you move forward when you feel stuck.

## Forgiveness and Appreciation Visualization

The following visualization can be read silently to yourself, or you can have someone read it to you. Reading it to soft music may help you relax. Sit in a comfortable chair as you go through this visualization, and hold your doll or bear.

*Settle comfortably into your chair. . . . If someone is reading to you, close your eyes. . . . Take some deep, relaxing breaths, and as you exhale, let all the tension go. . . . Notice which part of your body is most tight—legs, chest, shoulders, forehead. Breathe into it and just let go. . . . Let your shoulders drop, . . . let your jaw relax, . . . unclench your teeth, . . . let the chair support your body totally, . . . let your body be very relaxed.*

*Let your awareness go inward and see what you as an Adult Child do when you are feeling angry or hurt or scared or alone or in grief. How do you handle your difficult or painful feelings? Do you eat, take tranquilizers, drink, take drugs? Do you get angry and blame others for your feelings? Do you ignore your feel-*

*ings until they make you sick? Do you engage in some activity such as work or TV, hoping to blot out your feelings? Do you discount them as being silly or overreactive? Do you shame yourself for having these feelings, telling yourself that there is something wrong with you for your feelings? Do you caretake other people's difficult or painful feelings while ignoring your own? Do you stay stuck in misery and depression?*

*Now allow yourself to feel the Child within you. How do you as the Inner Child feel when your Adult Child ignores, shames, criticizes, discounts, caretakes, or blots out your feelings? Do you feel alone, anxious, unimportant, angry, depressed, scared, overwhelmed? Move inside your body and feel what it feels like to be alone within your body with no Adult there to love and care for you.*

*Now move back into your Adult Child and see your Inner Child—see how he or she feels when you are unloving to him or her.*

*Now speak to your Child and name one of the ways in which you are unloving to your Inner Child. . . .*

*Then become your Child, feel the hurt in you when your Adult Child is unloving to you, and tell your Adult Child about your anger and pain. . . .*

*Repeat this until you have told your Child all the ways you realize you are unloving to him or her, and your Child has responded with his or her feelings. Think of as many ways as you can that you have been unloving to your Child. Go as deep as you can with your eyes closed. . . . .*

*Now, as your Adult, speaking from your heart, share your sadness with your Inner Child for not knowing how to love him or her.*

*Now begin to look back on all the times you have acted unlovingly toward yourself, and know that you had good reasons for being unloving—that it all came from what you learned from the adults around you, and from your fears and false beliefs.*

*Put your focus into your heart and say to yourself, "I forgive myself for the unloving ways I've treated my Inner Child. I forgive myself for not knowing how to love myself. I forgive myself and now open myself to learning about how to love myself and others."*

*As you let that forgiveness in, feel it healing you inside and filling you up with peace. . . .*

*Now, from your loving Adult, let your Adult Child know that you appreciate his or her efforts to protect you from your pain. Say to your Adult Child,*

*"Thank you for being here for me all these years and trying your very best to help me not be in too much pain. I know you've always done the very best you could, and I want you to know I really appreciate all your efforts. Now it's time for you to just go back to being a child because I'm learning to be a loving Adult. I'm learning new ways to handle our pain. That means that you can relax and play and create and you no longer need to worry about handling things. I'm going to make sure that you feel loved and safe so that all that energy that goes into protecting can now go into learning and loving. I love you. Thank you again for all you've tried to do for me."*

*Feel your commitment to learn and love, to compassion and empathy rather than protection and avoidance. . . . And now hug your doll or bear.*

 *Celebrating Inner Bonding*

**D**oing the necessary work to create a loving Inner Bond between your Adult and your Inner Child and to heal the wounds of the past takes time and commitment. But the results make all the effort worthwhile. In fact, the results are nothing short of miraculous. A loving connection with our Inner Child creates the things we want most out of life:

• Connection to our Higher Power

• High self-esteem and a sense of wholeness

• Personal power (the soft power of power over ourselves, not the hard power of power over others)

• Inner peace and sense of safety

• Loving relationships

• Joy and passion

When we evaluate our actions—Step 6 of Inner Bonding—and find feelings of wholeness, peace, and joy within, we know we are loving ourselves.

## Connection to Our Higher Power

When the Adult and Child are lovingly bonded within, through our intent to learn and our willingness to take loving action, we are in our Higher Self, the channel through which flow the love and truths of our Higher Power.

## Self-Esteem and Wholeness

Self-esteem and a sense of inner wholeness are the result of our Adult loving our Inner Child. The more we learn to value who we really are, to take responsibility for our own feelings, wants, and needs, to behave lovingly in conflicts with others, the better we feel about ourselves. Our Inner Child will know he or she is important, lovable, and worthy only when our Adult treats that Child with love and respect. Through Inner Bonding, we learn that our best feelings do not come from outside ourselves, but from loving ourselves and others. This is what Inner Bonding is all about.

## Personal Power

Personal power is the power to make our own choices to realize our dreams. It is that inner experience of knowing that we can choose to heal our old pain, to take loving action to relieve present pain, and to bring about our joy. Inner Bonding moves us out of feeling like victims of other people's choices and into the power of our own choices.

## Inner Peace and Sense of Safety

We feel a sense of peace when our Adult and our Child are in harmony and when we are living in harmony with others and with the universe. Inner Bonding offers us the tools to resolve our inner and outer conflicts so that we can find that inner peace.

We feel safe when we have a loving Adult who takes care of us in the world, who makes sure we have what we need, and who stands up for us with others by setting appropriate boundaries.

## Loving Relationships

As we learn to love ourselves in the present and heal the wounds from the past, we will move away from the codependent behavior that erodes loving relationships and our relationships will become more loving and harmonious. Those who do not support our personal growth and highest good will likely fall by the wayside, and new, respectful, and supportive relationships will emerge. As we move from dependency into independence, we can attain the interdependence of a loving relationship.

## Joy and Passion

As we move into the intent to learn and open to feeling and healing our pain, we also open the door to our joy and passion.

In chapter 5 we listed some of the talents that people may be born with. As you open to knowing and loving your Inner Child, you'll find that you can get great joy from pursuing your talents. It may take quite a bit of time in developing the Inner Bond before your Child will let you in on his or her passions, but hopefully when that happens you will act on them. Filling out the following may help you become aware of some of the things that bring your Child joy. What are some of the things you've always wanted to do but have never gotten around to doing?

♪ I've always wanted to be involved in the following physical activities (check the ones that apply):

❏ Skiing, downhill

❏ Skiing, cross-country

❏ Snowmobiling

❏ Sledding, tobogganing

❏ Hiking

❏ Baseball

❏ Football

❏ Basketball

❏ Soccer

❏ Volleyball

❏ Ice hockey

❏ Water skiing

❏ Swimming

❏ Diving

❏ Gymnastics

❏ Bicycling, mountain biking

❏ Race-car driving, drag racing

❏ Horseback riding

❏ Running

❏ Cross-country running

❏ Walking

❏ Dancing, ballet

❏ Dancing, jazz

❏ Dancing, modern

❏ Dancing, ballroom

❏ Dancing, folk

❏ Dancing, square

❏ Aerobics

❏ Weight lifting, bodybuilding

❏ Self-defense, martial arts

❏ Flying, power planes

❏ Flying, gliders

❏ Paragliding

❏ Hot-air ballooning

❏ Skydiving

❏ Hang gliding

- ❏ Bungee jumping
- ❏ Windsurfing
- ❏ Surfing
- ❏ Parasailing
- ❏ Roller skating, roller blading
- ❏ Ice skating
- ❏ Skateboarding
- ❏ Scuba diving
- ❏ Snorkeling
- ❏ Bird-watching
- ❏ Boating, sailing
- ❏ Boating, powerboats
- ❏ Canoeing
- ❏ Kayaking
- ❏ River rafting
- ❏ Fishing
- ❏ Camping
- ❏ Backpacking
- ❏ Mountain climbing
- ❏ Rock climbing
- ❏ Target shooting
- ❏ Fencing
- ❏ Motorcycles, dirt biking
- ❏ Tennis
- ❏ Bowling
- ❏ Golf
- ❏ Racquetball, squash

❏ Badminton

❏ Lacrosse

❏ Rugby

❏ Archery

❏ Horseshoes

❏ Shuffleboard

❏ Croquet

❏ Travel

§ I've always wanted to take classes in or pursue on my own the following interests, creative activities, and hobbies:

❏ Astronomy

❏ Electronics

❏ Ham radio operation

❏ Singing

❏ Listening to music

❏ Composing or arranging music

❏ Playing an instrument

❏ Dancing

❏ Writing poetry

❏ Journaling

❏ Writing short stories

❏ Writing screen plays

❏ Writing novels

❏ Writing nonfiction

❏ Writing children's stories

❏ Writing letters

❏ Cooking

❑ Baking

❑ Cake decorating

❑ Canning

❑ Ice sculpture

❑ Drawing

❑ Painting

❑ Sculpture

❑ Computer art

❑ Cartooning

❑ Carving

❑ Ceramics

❑ Printmaking

❑ Photography

❑ Calligraphy

❑ Needlepoint

❑ Stained glass–making

❑ Beading

❑ Leatherwork

❑ Weaving

❑ Spinning

❑ Knitting

❑ Embroidery

❑ Crocheting

❑ Tie-dyeing

❑ Quilting

❑ Jewelry making

❑ Other crafts

- ❏ Building models—rockets, planes, boats
- ❏ Flying model planes or rockets
- ❏  Model railroading
- ❏ Acting
- ❏ Filmmaking
- ❏ Car repair
- ❏ Car restoration
- ❏ Gardening
- ❏ Horticulture
- ❏ Flower arranging
- ❏ Sewing
- ❏ Clothing design
- ❏ Playing board games
- ❏ Playing cards
- ❏ Video games
- ❏ Playing other games
- ❏ Raising animals
- ❏ Training animals
- ❏ Stamp collecting
- ❏ Coin collecting
- ❏ Rock collecting
- ❏ Rock hunting
- ❏ Other collections
- ❏ Woodworking
- ❏ Furniture making
- ❏ Furniture restoration
- ❏ Interior design

❏ Juggling

❏ Magic tricks

❏ Languages

❏ History

❏ Politics

❏ Public speaking

❏ Computer programming

❏ Psychology, Self-help

❏ Metaphysics

❏ Comparative religion

❏ Meditation

❏ Spirituality

❏ Nutrition

Community services:

❏ Environmental issues

❏ Work with the homeless

❏ Child abuse issues

❏ Battered women issues

❏ Animal rights

❏ Education

❏ Health research (cancer, AIDS, etc.)

❏ Care of the elderly

❏ Big Brothers, Big Sisters

❏ Hunger issues

❏ Civic organizations

❏ Hospital volunteering

❏ Hospice volunteering

❏ Prison volunteering

❏ Drug rehabilitation

❏ Political campaigns

If you are unhappy with your work, tuning into and pursuing your interests and talents can often lead to new possibilities for work.

Many of us had parents who told us that once we tried something, we had to stick with it, even if we didn't like it or got bored with it. This is very limiting: it is often difficult to try new things when we think we are permanently committed by our choices. To open the door to trying new things, we have to give our Inner Child permission to quit or to fail. We need to see quitting and failure as just a part of learning about what we want and don't want to do, can and cannot do, rather than as a black mark on our worthiness.

Allowing yourself to try new things without having to be stuck with them can often lead you into other things. One sport may lead to another that is more satisfying. One creative activity or interest can be a stepping-stone to others that eventually lead to new work or even a new life style. Staying open to learning about your passions and taking action on them is part of taking responsibility for your joy.

Have your beliefs and feelings about your Inner Child changed since you started this workbook? Go back to page 29 in chapter 2 and see what you wrote. What are your beliefs and feelings now?

_____

_____

_____

_____

_____

_____

_____

_____

_____

_____

## Visualization—Commitment and Connection

We end this workbook with a brief visualization that you can do when you feel you need some support in your commitment to loving your Inner Child.

This visualization can be read silently to yourself, or you can have someone read it to you. Reading it to soft music can help you relax. Sit in a comfortable chair as you go through this visualization.

*Settle comfortably into your chair. . . . If someone is reading to you, close your eyes. . . . Take some deep, relaxing breaths, and as you exhale, let all the tension go. . . . Notice which part of your body is most tight—legs, chest, shoulders, forehead. Breathe into it and just let go. . . . Let your shoulders drop, . . . let your jaw relax, . . . unclench your teeth, . . . let the chair support your body totally, . . . let your body be very relaxed.*

*Imagine a beautiful, warm, golden-white light above your head, the light of love and truth. Visualize that light coming into the top of your head and slowly moving down into your body, filling your whole body with the warm light of love and truth. Feel that light uniting you with all living beings, giving you a sense of harmony, reverence, and oneness with all life.*

*Say to yourself or say out loud: "I commit to loving my Child, to being in the intent to learn with my Child and my Higher Power, to dialoguing daily until the connection with my Child and my Higher Power is an ongoing one so that I am always in conscious connection with my Child's feelings and needs, and with the love and truth of my Higher Power. I commit to taking responsibility for my Child's feelings—for healing old wounds, for relieving present pain by taking loving action, and for taking action to bring my Child joy. I commit to creating a balance between work and play.*

*"I can soar, from this day forward, by creating the best for myself and offering the best of myself; by offering my hand first in friendship without losing my sense of self; by realizing that my dreams are special dreams that I offer to myself, my loves, and the planet. I commit, first and foremost, to becoming a loving Adult to my Inner Child and to becoming a loving human being with others and the planet."*

*Now open your eyes and give your Inner Child a hug.*